Streetwise Spycraft

This edition published by
Carlton Books
20 Mortimer Street
London W1T 3JW

ISBN 987-1-86200-461-0

Editorial Manager: Roland Hall
Project Art Editor: Darren Jordan
Design: Ben Ruocco
Illustrations: Peter Liddiard; Sudden Impact Media

The material in this book was previously published in *The Spycraft Manual*

Streetwise Spycraft

... protect yourself and learn the secret skills of twenty-first century espionage

SEVENOAKS

CONTENTS

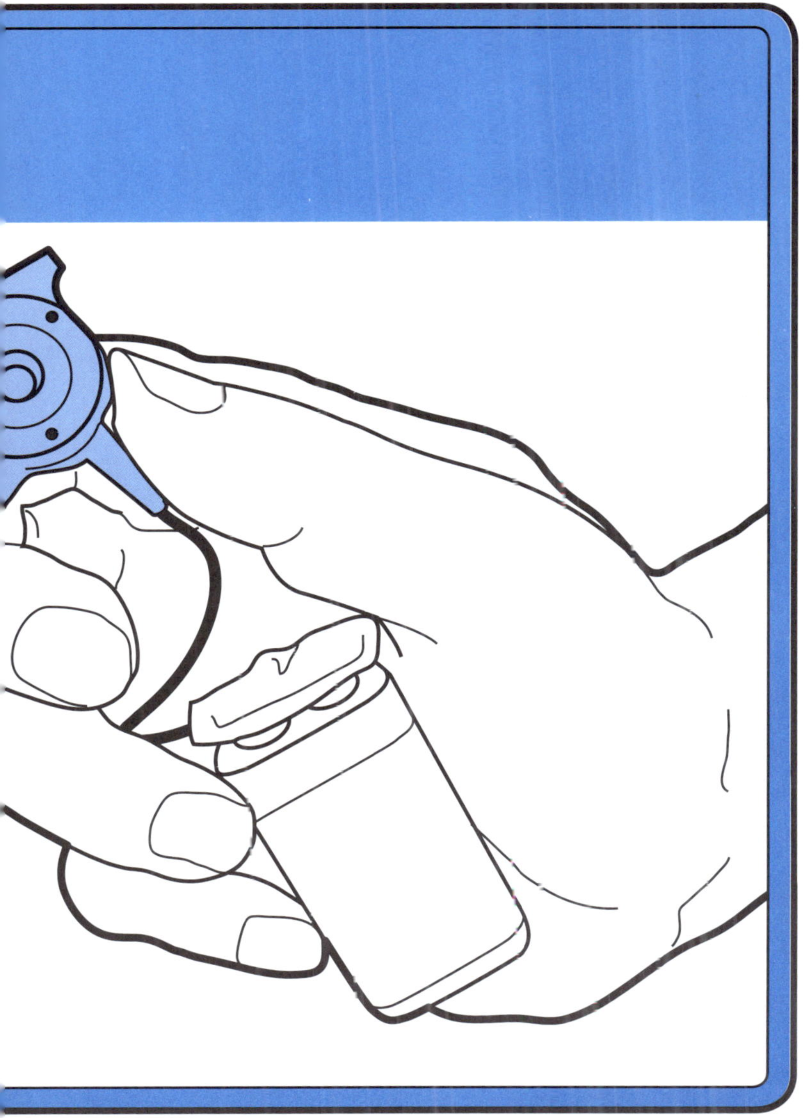

“Therefore, I say:

Know your enemy and know yourself;

in a hundred battles, you will never be defeated.

When you are ignorant of the enemy but know yourself,

your chances of winning or losing are equal.

If ignorant both of your enemy and of yourself,

you are sure to be defeated in every battle.”

Sun Tzu, *The Art of War,* c. 500bc

Introduction

Many years ago, my work as an SAS soldier took me to Northern Ireland. For the most part, my duties there consisted of undercover work and covert operation. With little guidance or support from the Security Service, we would identify and infiltrate those groups of people we believed to be involved in terrorist activities. Our techniques were honed through constant operations, which demanded skills such as lock picking, foot and vehicle surveillance and photography to name but a few. On the odd occasion we came across something really worthwhile, the Security Service in London would inevitability raise a lazy eye. My first contact with an MI5 agent did not create the best of impressions; he was unfit, overweight and, in terms of technical expertise, our own people were light years ahead. Things have changed since those days and today the SAS plays a large part in the day-to-day operation of the Security Service – for the most part doing the "dirty work".

After leaving the SAS, I pursued a career in counter-terrorism, a subject that has now become a goal for most of the western intelligence agencies. Therefore I decided to gather and distribute many of the techniques used by the world's leading intelligence agencies. I shall no doubt find myself in hot water for some of the material contained in this book. I am not overly worried, as I can prove that the majority is in the public domain – if you know where to look! My view is, "Why should the spooks have all the fun?" Where is it written that only spies should learn tradecraft?

The basic principle behind this manual is to demonstrate where the intelligence world stands today by describing the techniques and tradecraft skills used by most of the world's leading intelligence agencies. There is a limit to what I can write about, not for reasons of security, but based purely on the sheer magnitude of the subject. As a result, I have opted for a middle-of-the-road explanation that covers the main reasons for why we have spies and what a spy must learn in order to both survive and to be a good spy.

Some subjects, such as surveillance, are easy to categorize. Others, however, are individual and are more difficult to place within a structured framework. To combat this, I have included several topics as "pop-up" subjects that appear where I feel they are relevant. There are also several "case histories" that explain the reality of spying. Likewise, where applicable, I have indicated how the average person in the street can try their hand at some of the tradecraft subjects described in the book.

Streetwise Spycraft is a step-by-step instruction book on how spies learn their tradecraft and skills. Each individual subject contains masses of fascinating, hitherto largely undisclosed information, all of which is graphically illustrated. It covers subjects from the seven basic drills of agent contact to satellite surveillance and lock picking, making it a perfect reference for the world of espionage.

Finally, for better or worse, intelligence agencies will always be with us. They will always possess the means to delve deep into our innermost secrets. Let us hope that the sanctity of freedom, for which so many secret agents have died, rests consciously on the minds of those who currently control and direct covert operations.

Legal Implications

For the most part, the people who carry out daily surveillance operations – such as the police or private detectives – are governed by the basic laws of the country. While in theory this should be true of intelligence services, few countries act within the framework of either national or international law. Even when they have been exposed, many will do all everything in their power to annul the situation. To this end, I place no emphasis on the law and how it might affect the various intelligence agencies around the world.

1 SPIES

Intelligence agencies have existed in one form or another for centuries; their role was always to spy on each other. Much of that stopped in the early 1990s due to the disintegration of communism. By 2001, following the 9/11 attacks on the World Trade Center, a new enemy had been found – “Global Terrorism”.

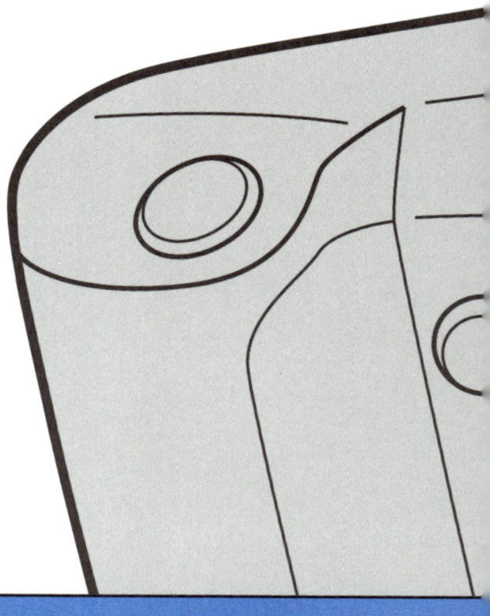

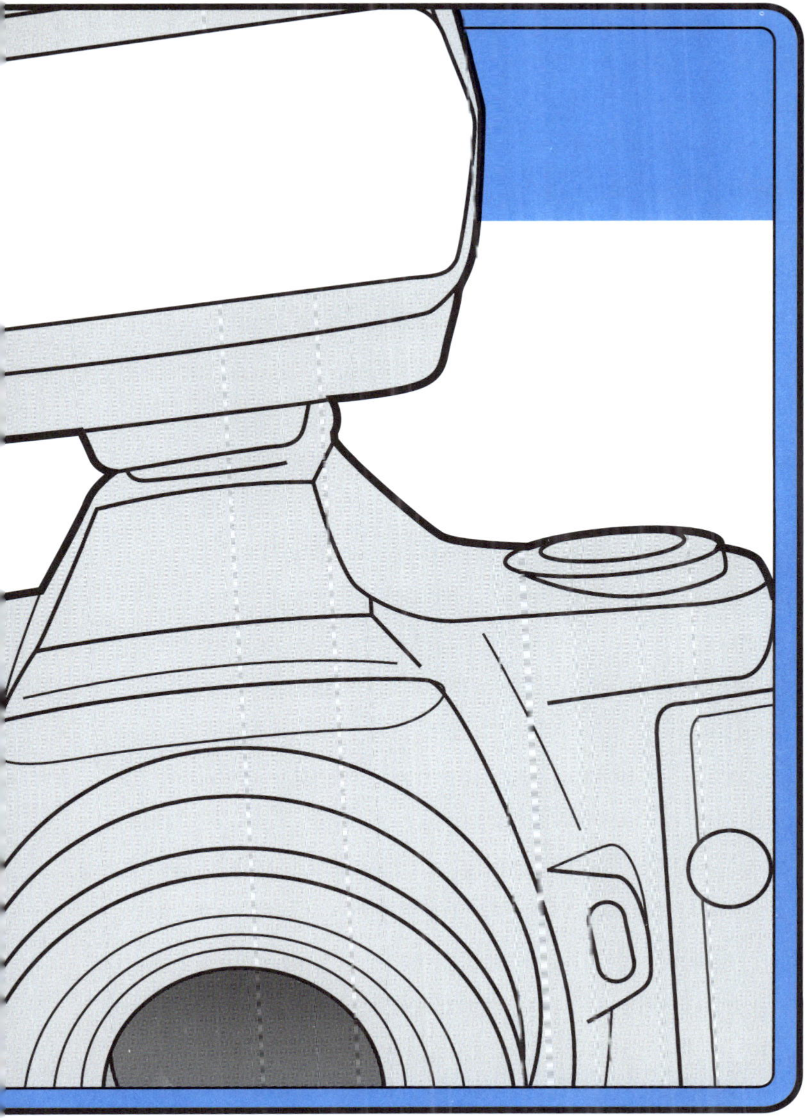

In the world of terrorism, knowledge is everything; without it there is very little chance of success. Although knowledge can be obtained through a number of sources, the primary method is through spying and surveillance. When the United States and the rest of the world were looking for the perpetrators of 9/11 and similar fiendish crimes, they could only be found through collecting and analyzing good intelligence.

Collecting intelligence involves human resource agencies (such as the CIA or MI5) and agencies who rely on eavesdropping and imagery (such as NSA, GCHQ, NRO and JARIC). In addition, embassies normally have an operating system from which they can establish information on a particular country. There is also the military. Finally, there is open information, obtained largely through the world's media. In some cases, this can be a far quicker means of obtaining information than via government agencies. In addition, there is normally a head of department, an official who follows the direction of their government. For example, the prime minister may pose the following question to his head of security: "Do we know who is responsible for last night's car bomb attack?"

The answer to this question is derived from information that has been gathered, interpreted and analyzed into intelligence. The intelligence is then distributed to those that decide what course of action is required.

Where do we start looking for information? First we look at those that have the capability and intent. Capability: "I know how to make a bomb from just about anything in the kitchen, but I have no intention of doing so, because it is dangerous and illegal." (I have the capability but not the intent). Intent: "I don't know how to make a bomb but as soon as I am able to, I will kill my neighbour." (I do not have the ability but I have the intention to commit harm.) Intelligence agencies are there to gather information about people who have both the capability and the intention. One of the principal threats currently facing the world is that of bioterrorism. Defending against such a threat and the vast devastation any biological attack could cause, governments are constantly on the lookout for terrorist organizations which have the capability to manufacture and deliver such weapons.

Who collects the information will depend largely on the enemy target and where that enemy is located. In most cases, several agencies will co-operate to achieve the same goal. Almost everyone is traceable. Individuals within the group use credit cards, mobile phones, vehicles, shipping, or may just be spotted walking down the street. Wherever they go, they can be tracked. Even terrorists living in remote areas can be found by the use of spy planes or satellite surveillance.

CIA

The Central Intelligence Agency was a late developer in terms of international espionage. Its predecessor, the Office of Strategic Services (OSS), was not formed until 1942. It officially became known as the CIA in 1947 after the National Security Act was passed and was charged with gathering, correlating, evaluating and disseminating intelligence affecting national security.

Reporting to the Senate Select Committee on Intelligence and the House Permanent Select Committee on Intelligence, most of its operational ability and efficiency can be held accountable by the State. At times, this leads to public accusations and damning criticism of its activities, especially in the case of the Iran-Contra affair and Watergate. Although CIA involvement in both cases was not proved, deep suspicion still remains as to its participation. However, its failures in the Bay of Pigs invasion of Cuba (1961), and more recently, the debacle over Saddam Hussein's missing weapons of mass destruction in Iraq, have proved damaging.

The headquarters of the CIA can be found on 258 acres of highly secured land at Langley, Virginia. Today it is divided into four specialist sections, or "directorates", all of which are concerned with the gathering and analysis of intelligence. In general, the CIA's sources are either manpower or hardware intensive and require huge amounts of funding.

The Directorate of Operations is responsible for gathering foreign intelligence by covert means and classical espionage. At least a quarter of the estimated 8,000 overseas staff include case officers responsible for running several thousand agents in other countries. The Directorate of Intelligence is concerned with the production of finished intelligence, whether in the form of quick-reaction briefings or long-term studies. The focus is worldwide, but the directorate is split into regional departments (African and Latin American; South and East Asian; European; Near Eastern; Slavic and Eurasian) as well as four offices that specialize in different types of analysis: resources, trade and technology; scientific and weapons research; leadership analysis and imagery analysis.

The Directorate of Science and Technology provides a supporting role to the CIA in terms of collecting and processing intelligence collected by covert technical means. This includes signals intelligence (SIGINT), imagery, satellite data and open source. The directorate is based on a separate site at Reston in Virginia and also includes the National Photographic Interpretation Center. It is estimated that there are about 26,000 staff employed here, including engineers, physicists, linguists, chemists, computer programmers and imagery analysts.

The final division is the Directorate of Administration. As its name implies, it provides administrative and technical support backup to the other facilities. It is also responsible for training field staff in espionage basics, such as lock picking, letter opening, etc. It is reported that about 1,000 personnel are employed within this directorate.

Since 9/11, the role of the CIA has become even more important in gathering intelligence to pre-empt any threat from militant Islamic terrorists such as Al Quaeda. Much criticism has already been levelled at the organization over whether or not warnings of a terrorist attack using aircraft were picked up and disseminated to the appropriate quarters of government before 9/11. In addition, the CIA was heavily lambasted over the weapons of mass destruction intelligence fiasco in Iraq. The Director of the CIA at the time, George Tenet, resigned – reportedly for reasons unconnected with Iraq. It remains to be seen whether the new director will restructure the organization or whether he will recruit more field staff to answer the growing threat of international terrorism.

MI5/MI6

Although military intelligence in England can be traced back to Elizabethan times, a dedicated service was not established until 1909, when MI5 and MI6 were created as internal departments under the control of the Secret Service Bureau.

Military Intelligence Department 5, under the control of Captain Vernon Kell, was then responsible for exposing German spies. MI6, under the command of Captain Mansfield Cumming, was in charge of gathering foreign intelligence. The responsibilities of MI5 grew in 1931 when it was charged with assessing all threats to national security and was given the title of the Security Service, although its previous name has remained in popular usage.

During the Second World War, MI6, now known as the Secret Intelligence Service (SIS) recruited and trained members of the Special Operations Executive (SOE), a force that became crucial to wartime intelligence gathering and sabotage behind enemy lines. At the end of the war, many of these operatives were reabsorbed into SIS.

Previously under the command of the military, both services later became divorced from the armed services. MI5 became the responsibility of the Home Secretary and MI6 reported to the Foreign and Commonwealth Secretary. Both organizations were issued with directives that defined their roles. MI5 today is still responsible for national security and counter-espionage activities, however it does not have the power to arrest suspects. This job falls to Scotland Yard's Special Branch, which is also responsible for the presentation of evidence at court on MI5's behalf. MI6's principal role is to provide intelligence gathered from foreign sources in support of national security, defence and foreign and economic policies.

Although traditionally rivals, both services have had to work together closely, especially when events exposed weaknesses in their operations. Scandals, such as the defection of British agents spying for the Russians (Burgess, MacLean and Philby) and the 1963 Profumo affair in which the Secretary for War of the time was caught sharing a high-class call girl with a Russian agent, created massive embarrassment for the services. Also, incidents such as the hijacking of the Iranian embassy in London in 1980 and the Libyan Peoples' Bureau in 1984, not to mention the "Troubles" in Northern Ireland, meant that the two services had to work together closely and share information in order to diffuse foreign threats on home ground.

Major changes took place in both services following the collapse of the Berlin Wall and the end of the Cold War. Staff numbers and budgets were reduced as it was deemed the threat from the Soviet Union was no longer so great. Arab terrorism still posed a danger, but the greatest danger now came from Northern Ireland, whose terrorists had increasingly taken their campaign onto the mainland. It is thought that many city-centre bombings, on the scale of the Manchester bombing in 1996, were averted as a result of having gained good intelligence.

After the Good Friday Agreement (1998), it seemed that yet another threat had been removed, but it was soon replaced by another, potentially far greater danger. Al Quaeda had always been a terrorist organization worth watching, but following the atrocities of 9/11, they suddenly became national security threat number one. Al Quaeda were not the only ones in the spotlight. Interest was also renewed in Iraq and its dictator, Saddam Hussein, following speculation that he possessed weapons of mass destruction. Both the security services in Britain and in the US claimed to have evidence to back up the accusation and it was on the strength of this evidence that the two countries and their allies went to war. In fact, as was established in the Butler Report in July 2004, it was clear that much of the so-called "intelligence" disclosed to the public was inaccurate. A lack of agents on the ground, second-hand intelligence and the claims of a few defectors who wished to see the overthrow of the regime, had all contributed to misleading claims about what Saddam actually possessed. Somehow and somewhere, between the intelligence agencies, the Joint Intelligence Committee (JIC) and Whitehall, suppositions became definites and hearsay became evidence. Although the Butler Report cleared anyone of purposely misleading Parliament and the public, it remains an embarrassing episode for the intelligence services, their bosses and perhaps, above all, Tony Blair.

Currently, the staffing level at MI5, based at Millbank in central London, is around 1,900. MI6, recently relocated to its new headquarters at Albert Embankment, is far more secretive about its employment figures, but one could safely assume that similar numbers to MI5 are involved, excluding those operatives in the field about whom nothing is known. Nevertheless, the threat from terrorism remains real enough. If anything concrete can be learned from the Butler Report it is that more spies are required and more intelligence about Al Quaeda and its allies needs to be gathered. This will probably lead to an escalation in recruitment for both MI5 and MI6.

KGB

KGB stands for Komitet Gosudarstvennoy Bezopasnosti, or The Committee for State Security. The most feared security service in the world, its first inception was created after the Russian Revolution in 1917.

Lenin's close ally Felix Dzerzhinsky took command of the old Tsarist secret police, the Okhrana, and reorganized and renamed it the CHEKA (Extraordinary Commission for Combating Counterrevolution and Espionage). The organization was renamed many times during the following years. From 1922–23 it was the GPU (State Political Administration) and from 1923–34 it became the OGPU (United States Political Administration). From there it changed to the NKVD (People's Commissariat for Internal Affairs) and then the MD (Ministry of Internal Affairs) and it only became known as the KGB in 1954.

Throughout its evolution, the organization developed a dreaded reputation, especially among its own people. During Stalin's reign, murderous thugs who were only too happy to carry out Stalin's often paranoid and bloody missions, headed the organization. For example, during the collectivization of land, the organization was responsible for the displacement and murder of millions of Russians.

The more familiar, modern-day form of the KGB only came about after Stalin's death in 1953. It became the most important part of the Soviet Union's intelligence service. As well as its own operations, it also oversaw the work of the GRU (Chief Intelligence Directorate of the General Staff of the Red Army), the military intelligence wing. It was extremely powerful; it was allocated a huge budget and possessed a staff that numbered in estimates from 500,000 to 700,000. Agents were not only involved in foreign espionage but also in domestic spying, with members secreted in every town and factory. Anyone considered to have views that ran counter to the party line was considered a traitor, was informed upon to be potentially dealt with by the KGB's SMERSH Division. This was a division within the secret service responsible for meting out punishments and assassinations to those considered to be an internal security threat.

During the Cold War, KGB agents targeted the western powers, especially top officials and military commanders with access to national secrets. Their favourite method involved the entrapment of an individual, usually through sexual temptations and blackmail. Another popular method was to employ listening devices in various foreign embassies.

The KGB's headquarters could be found at the infamous Lubyanka Square in downtown Moscow. The huge, intimidating building was once feared but in later years it has been opened up to public inspection, thanks to the intervention of successive presidents from Yuri Andropov – a former KGB chief who was president between 1982-1984 – onwards.

Since the collapse of the Soviet Union, the KGB has been on a rocky road. In 1991, certain sections of the KGB Spetsnatz forces attempted to storm the Russian parliament building and force a coup against president Mikhail Gorbachev and other senior politicians. However, once there, some of the forces refused to take part and so helped the coup to fail. The ringleaders were arrested and, in October 1991, Gorbachev signed a decree abolishing the KGB. Since then, most of its directorates have continued through separate organizations – though its direct successor successor agency, the Federal Security Service of the Russian Federation (FSB) also performs many of the functions of the former KGB.

It is interesting to note that the current president of Russia, Vladimir Putin, is also a former chief of the KGB. Today, Russia's security forces are more concerned with the fight against global and internal terrorism, especially that issuing from Chechnya and other former Soviet states.

Mossad

Mossad, the shortened form of its full Israeli name – ha Mossad le-Modin ule-Tafkidim Meyuhadim (The Institute for Intelligence and Special Tasks) – is Israel's powerful and secretive intelligence agency.

It was formed by Israel's prime minister, David Ben Gurion, in 1951, with the primary directive: "For our state, which since its creation has been under siege by its enemies, intelligence constitutes the first line of self-defence ... We must learn well how to recognize what is going on around us." The name Mossad was appropriate for an institution responsible for the defence of Israel as it was also the name of an organization that, during the 1930s and 1940s, helped to smuggle thousands of Jewish refugees into Palestine.

Mossad is responsible for gathering intelligence as well as conducting secret operations connected with national security and counter-terrorism. Due to the conflicts Israel has had with its neighbours, much of its focus is on the Arab nations and, in particular, the activities of terrorist organizations such as Hamas and the PLO. However, it also conducts espionage and intelligence activities throughout the world and is still involved with the undercover movement of Jewish refugees from hostile countries, such as Ethiopia, Iran and Syria. It currently provides the West with information on the movement of known Arab terrorists and has excellent relations with corresponding western intelligence agencies, in particular with the CIA.

The headquarters of Mossad are in Tel Aviv. Details about employee numbers are hard to obtain, but it is estimated that between 1,200 and 1,500 work there. The "Institute" is headed by a director – currently Meir Dagan – who is only responsible to the prime minister. In line with its importance to the State of Israel, Mossad has a huge budget and, in contrast to other foreign intelligence agencies, also has the power to deal with countries with which Israel has no diplomatic relations. Its inner organization, although obscure, has at least eight known departments.

The largest of these is the Collections Department, which is responsible for espionage operations. It possesses offices in other countries – both acknowledged and unacknowledged – which are in charge of directing and recruiting agents. The Political Action and Liaison Department is in charge of communications with the foreign intelligence services of other countries as well as countries with which Israel does not normally engage. It is also responsible for political activities. The Special Operations Division is perhaps the one most often thought of when Mossad is mentioned. It is responsible for extremely covert actions such as assassination, sabotage and paramilitary activities. Also known by its other name, Metsada, one of its duties is to track down individuals who have harmed Jewish people in any country. Also linked to this department is Mossad's special army unit known as the "Sayaret Matkal", or General Staff Reconnaissance Unit. This secretive force, known colloquially as "The Guys" number about 200 men and are responsible for many of the covert actions that take place.

The Research Department handles the analysis of intelligence, providing daily, weekly and monthly reports. It is organized into 15 geographical desks: the US; Canada and Western Europe; the former Soviet Union; Africa; Latin America; China; the Mahgreb (Morocco, Algeria and Tunisia); Saudi Arabia; Syria; Jordan; Iran; the United Arab Emirates; Iraq and Libya. There is also a "nuclear desk" concerned with weapons of mass destruction. The Technology Department researches and develops technologies that might be useful to Mossad and the LAP (Lohamah Psichologit) Department handles all propaganda and psychological warfare operations.

It is worth mentioning that many of Israel's top politicians and leaders began their working lives within the ranks of Mossad: Yitzhak Shamir, Menachem Begin and Yitzhak Rabin had all been, at one time or another, part of the Mossad organization.

The Spy

The dictionary describes a spy as (i) a person employed by a state or institution to obtain secret information from rival countries, organizations or companies; or (ii) a person who keeps watch on others.

However, this simple explanation does not come close to explaining the real complexities that make up the modern spy. Today's spy is far removed from the James Bond image we see on our cinema screens. Gone are the classical military and political intelligence agents that fight against enemy or rival states. The dinner jacket has been replaced by a bullet-proof vest worn underneath shabby clothes. If there is any comparison between fiction and reality, it is in the world of Q, for today's spy is equipped with state-of-the-art electronic wizardry.

Intelligence in the field of counter-terrorism is a different and, in many aspects, more arduous and dangerous task. The lives of many agents are in continual danger. The rules of the game are cruel as moral and ethical considerations are simply negated by the bullet. There is no honour between rivals on the streets of Kabul or Baghdad and only the quick survive. A modern spy must blend in, live among the enemy, speak their language and befriend and exploit the enemy at every opportunity. They are required to be streetwise, rough, tough and deadly.

All spies receive some form of basic military training. This involves learning how to fire a variety of weapons, self-defence and resistance to interrogation should they get caught. After the basic training, some spies are trained in the arts of surveillance, while others become technical officers, but by far the most dangerous job is that of the field officer. One vital role for this type of spy is to recruit local agents, people he can use to his advantage, people who will happily kill for him. Finding such people is the key to success in any intelligence operation. First and foremost the field officer must identify the right person, someone who is in a position or has the skills to carry out his dirty work. Once he has found such a person he must go about recruiting them, discovering their weakness and exploiting it. In many instances, a field agent will be responsible for recruiting and running several agents at the same time, none of which will know of the others existence.

In the West, spies are trained and controlled by massive organizations such as the CIA or MI5. These provide the spy with technical support, and when required, hard back-up with a call on the full weight of military intervention. For the most part, however, spying is a lonely, shadowy game, fraught with danger. For this reason, the modern spy must learn all the basics of tradecraft. For example, in the United Kingdom, spies go through a procedure known as the Intelligence Officers' New Entry Course (INOEC). This course takes place in various parts of the country, including the Fort at MI6's training establishment in Portsmouth, and the SAS base at Credenhill, Hereford.

What Makes a Good Spy?

One of the first skills a spy must have is good observation. No matter where he or she is or what they are doing, their mind should be systematically recording places, events and people, with great recall accuracy. The military have a lesson on this subject. They place a number of objects in an area some metres away from trainees. They are given a short period of time in which to observe all the objects before they are taken away. They are not allowed to write them down for several hours.

Try doing the same when you enter a room for the first time, or spot a car number plate. Register the number of windows in the house you just passed. The trick is to keep as much information in your brain for as long as possible. Like most subjects, the more you practice the better you become at it.

Use logic to understand things. How did they do that? How can I do this? What if I go in totally the opposite direction, not just physically but mentally? Is there another way to solve this situation? Try some lateral thinking.

Adjust your attitude to the situation. Think before you react. What do people expect of you? What is your role model to be? It is no good pretending to be a bag lady if you are dressed like a princess. The weak have always been taken advantage of – if the situation allows, take control and assert yourself. Be interested in people, this takes the focus off yourself. Most people are only too happy to boast about their social position, wealth, family or occupation, so take advantage of this. "That sounds interesting, it must be a wonderful job," will open up a conversation that could deliver lots of useful information. Play on people's emotions: "I have just broken up with my girlfriend, she went off with another woman." Your comment will get you both sympathy and inquisition into your ex-girlfriend's sexual habits. Another good opener in recruiting a possible agent is: "I have just won the lottery – not all of it, but a good sum."

Learn to listen to your sixth sense or to analyze any gut feeling you might get. There are many basic instructions in the human brain that warn us of danger – learn to recognize them and take appropriate action. You may walk down a street and spot the same person you saw only an hour ago in a different part of the city – is this just a coincidence?

Only ever take calculated risks, never be a gambler. With a calculated risk you can spot the drawbacks and adjust your plans accordingly. Always analyze your actions and base your actions on solid information. If you take a gamble, you only need to fail once. Here are a few tips:

- **Always be aggressive in a dangerous situation, because you can guarantee that the enemy will be. Let them know you are not to be messed with – get your punch in first.**
- **Know your own strengths and weaknesses.**
- **Know your territory and its inhabitants.**
- **It is better to be known than to be a stranger to the area and its inhabitants. Let your cover story protect you.**
- **Know when to get out and always have an escape route planned.**
- **When the situation goes horribly wrong and you get caught – never give up.**

The Cover Story

The one thing that must stand up in the world of spying is the spy's cover story. They must be who they say they are and when working in a foreign country, be able to prove their identity.

By far the best way of obtaining a cover story is to make it as near to the truth as possible; details such as your age and place of origin, your education, and your likes and dislikes, for example. By doing so, you do not fall into a trap when an enemy intelligence agency starts an in-depth background check into your life.

Many spies enter a foreign country as part of the embassy staff or as part of a diplomatic mission. In some countries, the role of the Defence Attaché is little short of a spymaster. His position will not allow him to partake in direct actions, but he will act more as an umbrella for a network of spies and agents working on behalf of his country. Spies are recruited by a government from time to time simply because they have the right qualification. They could, for example, be a businessman who has just won an order into a foreign country. This grants him an automatic cover story and a legitimate reason for travelling. However, both of the above examples are restricted, firstly by protocol and secondly by a lack of espionage training. The real answer is to train a potential spy in the arts of tradecraft and provide him with a believable cover story.

Recruiting

Spies work for the intelligence services of their respective countries. They see themselves as either case officers or field officers, both of which are commonly referred to as "handlers". They rarely go into a foreign country and do the dirty work themselves.

When a spy is operating in a foreign country, the best way to gather information is to recruit local agents. The basic plan is to get these agents to steal anything for you while never disclosing the spy's true identity. Once an agent is recruited properly, the spy can use them for just about anything: soliciting vital information, sabotage, deception, covert operations, assassination and sex. While this might sound a little outlandish, you must keep in mind that the recruitment machinery of most intelligence agencies is built on lies, deception and, above all, using people.

Most recruited agents are classified as either "primary" or "access". A primary agent will have direct access to what it is the spy requires, while an access agent is a go-between. When the operation is in the planning stages, a certain amount of money will be allocated to the handler to recruit agents and, in order to recruit several agents, the spy will need extra funding. The money may come from the intelligence agency budget, or be self-generating from the operation, i.e. the sale of weapons or drugs. Money can buy most things, like friendship, favours, sex and drugs, although the latter may well be directly supplied by the intelligence agency. However, the best tool a handler can have is the ability to tell totally believable lies.

Potential Agents

The first task of the handler is to spot his intended agent. That means finding people who have access to the information he requires.

He may initially select several people and then narrow down his list accordingly. He will look for the lonely secretary or the disgruntled employee. The potential target may be a computer programmer or a code-breaker, but it would be better to recruit an analyst, as they have access to more information. Soft potential targets include:

- **People with a careless security attitude or a grudge.**
- **Defectors who have fled their own country.**
- **Detainees or prisoners who will work for a reduced sentence.**
- **Foreign agents who have been caught and "turned". These are known as "double agents".**
- **People who can be threatened or blackmailed.**
- **Those who might be tempted by financial reward.**

Once the handler has spotted someone in a position that best serves his interests, he must find a way to make them co-operate. First he must decide how he is going to make the initial contact. When doing so he must be careful to put some form of security and safety measures in place before approaching the new agent.

Having chosen his prospective agent, the handler must then evaluate them, test them and finally train them to do his dirty work.

The evaluation process is used to determine an agent's reliability and their capability to produce the required information. This process starts off with the initial contact between the handler and the agent. The handler will get to know the agent and will be looking to discover any weaknesses that will help. By this time the handler will have perfected his cover story and will be in full flow as to why he is in the country, where he lives and what work he does. He will also act a little superior, as if his job is extremely important. As the relationship becomes more refined, and after a degree of trust has been established, the handler will start providing little favours to the agent. If the handler has done his homework, he will know roughly how much the potential agent earns, from this he can deduce both his living conditions and his lifestyle needs. These rewards will then be increased, but always in a safe and logical way so that the agent does not become suspicious. When the moment comes to ask the agent to risk obtaining information for the handler, he will not depend solely on monetary rewards; a second and third option, such as blackmail, will be in place. At this stage in the recruitment process, the agent suddenly becomes aware of the trap he has fallen into; he has betrayed his country, his employer, his friends and his family. This is where the handler's cover story can come in useful, as it will allow him to add some lies to ease the agent's conscience. If the prospective agent categorically refuses to co-operate and indicates that he will go to the authorities, the handler must consider killing the agent.

Once the handler has hooked the agent, he will start the testing phase, effectively checking that the agent is capable of delivering the required information. If this proves successful, then the agent's training will begin. During this phase, the handler will instruct the agent how to make contact and how to avoid being followed. The agent will be shown how to construct and mark a dead-letter drop, and how to use a variety of equipment in order to help solicit the information, such as miniature cameras. If the agent is being used for sex, they will then be instructed in the use of covert recording equipment. The handler rarely provides the agent with guns or explosives; it may well provide the agent with a means of getting rid of him should things go wrong. In all cases, the handler will do his best to stick with his cover story and will continue to be as friendly as possible with the agent while continuing with the monetary rewards. If the handler thinks that the agent is getting too close to him and that operational security is at risk, then he may well pass the agent on to another handler. It is vital that the agent never gets the chance to break off contact and they can never be allowed to quit or resign.

Sex can be a useful tool during the recruitment stage. It can be used to coerce someone to turn traitor or it can help manipulate someone into a compromising position. In many cases, sex can be a more effective tool than money, alcohol or drugs. Heterosexual compromise is used by many of the world's intelligence agencies. This starts with a simple introduction, i.e. putting a glamorous-looking woman in the same room as the target. One thing leads to another, with the end result being compromising photographs. The same applies with homosexuals; the beautiful woman is simply replaced by a pretty boy. Not all "honey traps", as they are commonly known, rely on photographs; the woman may say she is pregnant or the young boy may declare that he has AIDS. Both will be untrue, but they will serve to put extra pressure on the target.

A non-sexual compromise could come in a variety of disguises, such as criminal actions or security violations. The handler will exploit any of the handler's known compromises. If the promising agent has a clean past, the handler may well stage an event in which the agent is alleged to be a guilty party. Witnesses will be found, normally other agents under the handler's control, to provide evidence that proves the proposed agent to be guilty.

Whatever method the handler uses to co-opt the services of the agent, once achieved he must also provide some basic tradecraft training. It is in the handler's interests to make the agent as security minded as possible and to ensure that the required objectives are being carried out correctly. In order to keep the agent firmly on his side, the handler must make sure that he can deliver any monetary or other favourable promises. The agent's sole purpose is to do the bidding of the handler. Where this requires technical assistance, the handler must supply the agent with the necessary equipment and teach him how to use it. The recruitment of an agent is a long and dangerous game. Bearing this in mind, a good agent will need to be protected, even if this means that the handler has to prove assistance in any emergency.

DOUBLE AGENTS

When a spy enters a foreign country it is always possible that they have been recognized and put under surveillance. Instead of picking the spy up, the foreign agency may wish to keep them under surveillance and even try to plant a double agent. This double agent, commonly referred to as a "mole", will put themselves in a position where they can be recruited by the spy. A classic mole is one who has been recruited by the spy and then discovered by the opposition. When discovery is a choice between death or being a double agent, then the latter is often preferred.

For this reason the spy must ensure that anyone he recruits is genuine and test them accordingly. This testing phase is normally done by a specialist counterintelligence officer. This person will know how to detect and neutralize attempted penetrations by enemies of your organization. This normally means feeding some sensitive information to the new recruit – and only to the recruit. It is simply a matter of waiting to see if this information comes to light from another source. For this reason it is best not to overuse new recruits until they have proved themselves.

Agent Contact

Once a spy has recruited his agent, he will need to meet him in order to issue instructions and to collect intelligence. This procedure is called "agent contact". Under normal circumstances, a handler working in a foreign country must assume that he is under surveillance.

In order to set up a clandestine meeting with the agent, he will go through a set of procedures to ensure that an enemy surveillance team is not observing the meeting. Both the handler and the agent will have previously agreed upon a place, a date and a time or they will have set up a signal that indicates a meeting is to take place. In addition, they are familiar with each other's appearance, i.e. they can recognize each other on sight. The handler will provide the agent with a set of unique communication codes; this may be defined by hand signals, actions or clothing. The agreed signals will have various meanings such as, "We need to talk" or "I am under surveillance". A normal meeting between a handler and an agent would follow these basic steps.

STEP ONE

Both arrive independently at the previously agreed general location. Rather than fixing a specific location, they agree to be only in the general vicinity. This is an important principle. In this example, they are using a large park in a residential district. The location is free of video surveillance cameras. Ideally, the location should also be out of range of telephoto lenses. Other locations could include bus stops or a convenience store.

STEP TWO

Both the handler and the agent make discreet eye contact at some distance from each other. The handler, being the senior of the two, may use a prearranged signal to tell the agent that he has spotted him, such as moving a newspaper from one hand to the other or lighting a cigarette. The signal must be a movement that does not attract the unwanted attention of any enemy surveillance operators. It is important for both players at this carry out their surveillance with just one or two people; they literally surround their target with very large numbers.

STEPS ONE & TWO

STEP THREE

STEP FOUR

STEP FIVE

STEP THREE

Once the recognition signal has been established, the handler will simply walk off leaving the agent to follow at a distance. This ensures that the handler is clean and that he has not grown a tail. Surveillance teams on foot work on what is called a "floating-box principle". This means that they would form a very loose formation around the subject they are following. All main entry and exit points to a particular location will also be covered.

STEP FOUR

When the agent has satisfied himself that the handler is clean, he will make a signal to him. This will usually be the carrying out of some everyday task, such as re-tying his shoelaces. Now the roles are reversed, this time the handler follows the agent to establish that he is also "clean".

STEP FIVE

When the handler is satisfied that neither he nor the agent are under surveillance, he will give the signal to meet. On the other hand, if either the handler or the agent suspects that a surveillance team is in the vicinity, they will simply abort the operation and walk away. Once they meet, they will discuss any issues and agree upon the date, the time and the location of their next clandestine meeting. This will also include several back-up plans in case that meeting is thwarted by surveillance.

Surveillance – Trust Your Instincts

It is vitally important to trust your instincts, because if something appears to be suspicious it is better to be safe than sorry. Many people are surprised to learn that it is not difficult to detect a surveillance team. If the agent requests a meeting with his handler, the latter must be careful that he is not being set up. Such a request by the agent is known as a "blind date".

Passing Messages

Messages can be passed in any number of ways. They can be done visually, in order to avoid contact association between the handler and the agent, or they can be covertly delivered. Over the years, both handlers and agents have devised numerous ways of passing messages. I have outlined a number of different techniques below:

Hollow Coin

Every country in the world has a currency system in place in order for the population to carry out their daily business, such as buying food, eating in cafes or paying for everyday goods. This is a natural transaction and one that is exploited by spies. Say that the handler needs to meet with his agent. He walks down the street and buys a newspaper, or stops for a coffee. The very action of buying a newspaper or a coffee requires that money change hands. If the newsagent or waiter is the contact, what better way to pass a message?

Tip – You can get your own hollow coin by purchasing one from a store which sells magic tricks.

A Dead-Letter Box (DLB)

A dead-letter box is commonly referred to as a "DLB". It is a precise place where a message, or any other material, can be covertly left by one person and be collected by another. The aim of the DLB is to transfer a message without either parties making contact; and thus avoiding being observed by others. The DLB can be located in almost any place providing that the placement and the pick-up can be carried out naturally. Placing a container in the ground, under a park bench or in a trash can have all been used. The secret of a good DLB is ingenuity.

DLB Procedure

While each country has its own methods for teaching DLB procedures, the one devised and perfected by the KGB is the best example of how it should be done. Providing both the sender and receiver have proficient skills in counter-surveillance techniques, conforming to the KGB method will guarantee safe delivery.

The DLB Location

Find a good location where you are temporarily unsighted by any surveillance team. Choose your spot either to fill or to insert a DLB position or a container. Always choose a location that is populated, such as a park or public transport, and avoid isolated places. Find places close to the DLB, but far enough away to avoid suspicion, where you can leave a signal that either the DLB is ready for filling, that there is material in the box and that the material has been picked up. These signals should be foolproof and unspotted by any surveillance team.

Several DLB places should be known and agreed by both the handler and the agent. Likewise, a timing system should be in place for each DLB drop. The time spent in the area should be limited and the pick-up should never take more than 15 minutes. To increase security for a DLB, the handler and agent should have a number of fake DLB locations. These should be worked into the handler's or the agent's normal daily routine. All the handler and the agent have to do is to walk past these fake DLBs on a regular basis.

STEP ONE: READY-TO-FILL SIGNAL

You have made your delivery device and intend to pass the information on to your handler. Assuming that a predetermined area has been agreed on, the first step is for the agent to signal that he his "ready to fill" the DLB. This might take the form of a chalk mark or a piece of chewing gum stuck on a park bench. The idea is to produce a signal that can be seen clearly but which is virtually imperceptible to the general public's eye.

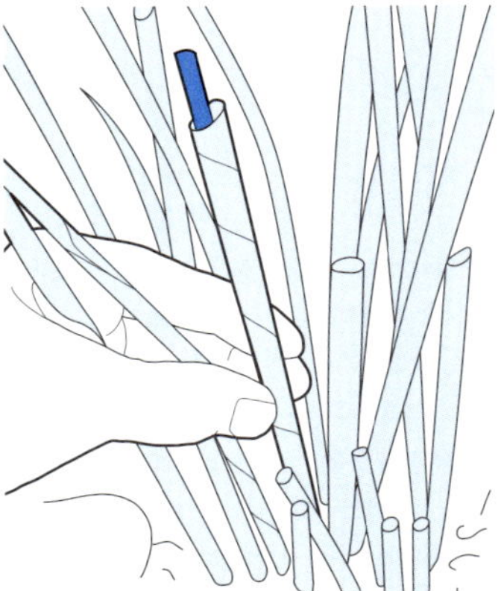

STEP TWO: READY-TO-PICK-UP SIGNAL

Once the handler sees the ready-to-fill signal, he will make a ready-to-pick-up signal. As with the agents "ready-to-fill" signal, this will normally involve something simple, such as lighting a cigarette or making a chalk mark. On seeing this, the agent will place or fill the DLB. Once this task has been done, the agent will then remove his ready-to-fill signal. By doing so, he is simply informing the handler that the material is in the DLB.

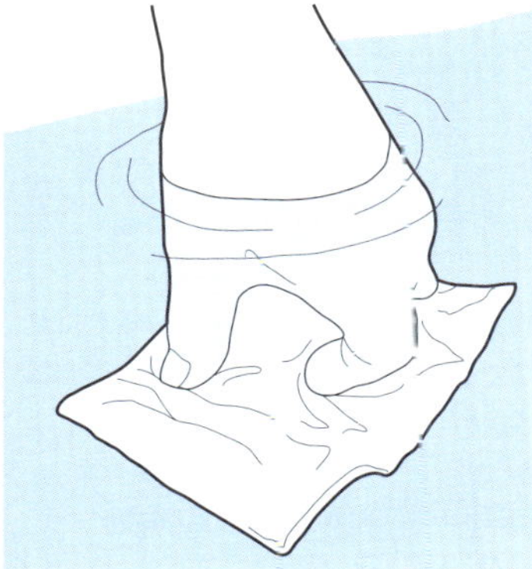

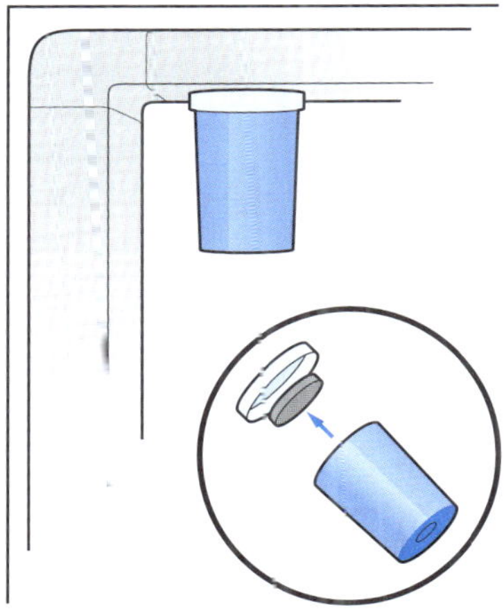

STEP THREE: ALL-CLEAR SIGNAL

Only when the handler has seen the agent remove the ready-to-fill signal will he approach the DLB and collect the message. He will remove his own ready-to-pick-up signal the moment he has recovered the message. This tells the agent that he has recovered the message and that the DLB is now empty.

At this stage both the handler and the agent will leave the area. In the event that the handler has not shown up within the prearranged time, the agent will simply remove his ready-to-fill signal.

How to Make Your Own DLB

The trick to creating a good DLB rests in coming up with something unobtrusive that blends in well with its location. A straw matching the bed of reeds it will planted in makes a good receptacle for a message. A watertight plastic snack wrapper holding a message, submerged a couple of inches under the surface of a pond can easily be collected – the action of picking it up appearing to be that of a citizen concerned about litter. Using a magnet under the lid of an empty photographic film canister is a good way of attaching a DLB to the metal underside of a park bench.

2 SECRET CODES

While messages can be passed covertly between the handler and the agent, there is always the possibility that the opposition might detect the exchange and intercept the message. To this end, all messages should be coded in one form or another. Many ingenious devices have been used over the years to enable governments, the military and spies to pass messages. In order for a coding system to be truly unbreakable, it must work in an unstructured way, in other words, randomly. The development of the One-Time Pad (OTP) went a long way to achieving this goal. Perfected in 1917 during the First World War, OTP consists of random keys (number blocks) with the whole making a pad. These numbers are used only once, hence the name. OTP is the only cipher system that cannot be cracked and is used for secret communications by just about all of the world's major intelligence agencies.

YZABCDE
STUVWXYZABCDEFGHIJKLM

Sample OTP

The following is a sample page from a one-time pad. The numbers are generated by random selection; the pad is numbered, as is the page and the line.

There are only ever two copies of the OTP, one with the intelligence agency and the other with the field agent. The intelligence agency's copy is normally kept by the cipher operator; someone who works in a high security building, thus ensuring the safety of the copy. Very few people have access to the "pad", neither do they know which agent is using which pad. Only the ciphered message is passed up for intelligence analysis. The field agent will have the second copy. If he is compromised then he will destroy his pad in a special wallet that burns the pad in seconds. Even when the enemy has managed to get their hands on an agent's pad, there are simple checks that can be put in place to confirm authenticity. If the intelligence agency has the slightest suspicion that their agent has been compromised, they will automatically destroy their pad.

PAD 5 - PAGE 17

01	25271	39210	42651	87192	46617	38194	42769	91808	31347	53927
02	69221	67841	74189	24875	01928	04079	88107	39658	80219	52768
03	87301	36533	61098	67823	56430	78871	23310	90312	47820	22495
04	43278	54309	87663	56563	09823	45656	87503	44596	23320	24319
05	39221	67841	74189	24875	01928	04079	88107	39658	80219	52768
06	65271	39210	42651	87192	46617	38194	42769	91808	31347	53927
07	93278	54309	87663	56563	09823	45656	87503	44596	23320	24319

There are many ways in which a numbered code can be deciphered into a simple language. This can either be achieved by starting at a random place in the alphabet triggered by a number or through the use of a common book, such as an encyclopaedia.

The most common form is to have a "vocab" book that lists a simple set of names and special letters and which will also provide the user with an alphabet from which he can spell place names that are not in the vocab book.

We can now translate the following message using the vocab book below and then encrypt it using the OTP:

AGENT WILL MEET YOU AT GR327903 2 PM 5 AUGUST.
HE WILL GIVE YOU WEAPONS AND AMMUNTION.

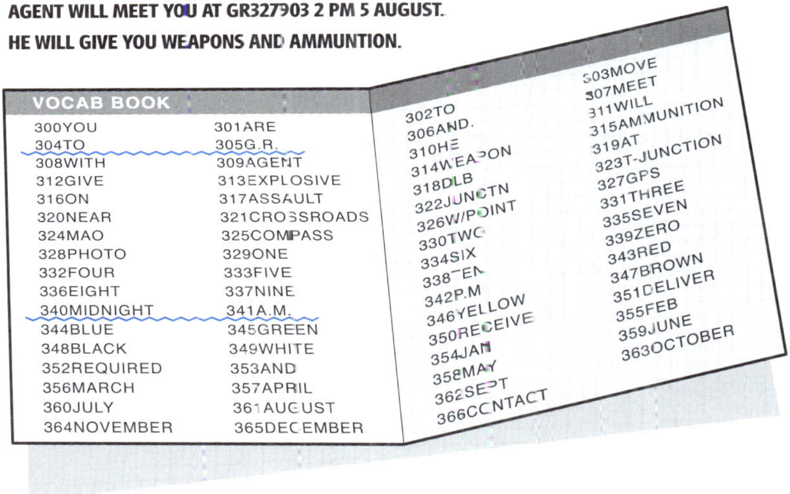

STEP ONE

Find the word agent in the vocab book and write down the three-digit number next to it, i.e. 309Agent. Continue to do this until you have written down all of the digits. Any numbers in the message are simply left unchanged. You should finish up with the following line of numbers, which you should then separate into a block to match those in the codebook, in this example blocks of five:

30931 13073 00319 30532 79032 34253 61310 31131 23003 14306 31516

STEP TWO

Choose a line to start in your codebook, in this example we have used line three, and place the number block taken from the vocab book under those in the codebook. Next subtract without carrying units forward.

Line one = codebook, line two = vocab book and line three = the subtracted numbers.
87301 36533 61098 67823 56430 78871 23310 90312 47820 22495 43278
30931 13073 00319 30532 79032 34253 61310 31131 23003 14306 31516
57470 23560 61789 37391 87408 44628 62000 69281 24827 18191 12762

STEP THREE

Next add the codebook number, page and line to the front of the subtracted numbers i.e.
(51703) 57470 23560 61789 37391 87408 44628 62000 69281 24827 18191 12762

These numbers can now be safely transmitted to the agent; they will make absolutely no sense to an enemy unit even if they manage to intercept them.

STEP FOUR

Once the agent has received the message he uses the first block to identify the correct codebook, page and start line. (Agents may well have several different codebooks using one for each person they deal with.) The agent has the only other copy of the OTP code book, so it is a simple matter of placing the received message, less the indicator block, under the correct line and subtracting the numbers. The subtracted numbers are then broken down into blocks of three in order to find the message from the vocab book.

Creating an OTP Pad

Making your own OTP pad and vocab book is easy. Once completed, simply make one extra photocopy and give it to your friend. You can now exchange messages in total secrecy.

Spot Codebook

The spot code system can be used either by spies, agents or surveillance operators.

It is a particularly good system as it allows the user to identify a major feature, usually a specific place, junction or crossroads. When a spot code system is used for surveillance, it allows the desk operator to know where all the surveillance operators are at all times. He can also direct foot and vehicle surveillance to a specified spot.

When used by handlers and agents, the spot code system offers several automatic back-up options. For example, if "blue 5" is compromised, both the handler and the agent will automatically know that they have to meet at "blue 6" and so on. This is how it works:

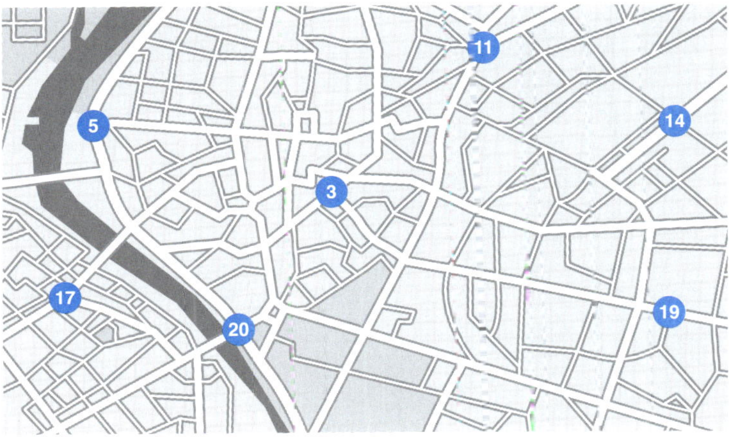

A SIMPLE SPOT CODE

A spot code is normally made by allocating a colour and a number to each major road intersection. As the surveillance operator drives from one intersection to another, he simple identifies himself and tells the desk operator. "Nine this is Sierra Papa four – towards blue 5'30–35." When driving, the operator simply adds the approximate speed to the end of his call, providing a rough estimated time of arrival at the next spot. When the area is new to the operator, he will carry a spot codebook in his vehicle. However, should this codebook fall into enemy hands, it will present a short-term security risk. This will result in all the spot codes being changed and with everyone having to learn the new codes.

The spot code system can also be used to refer to actions rather than a location. This helps throw the enemy off balance should they be watching them or listening to the operation. For example: "Sierra Papa four – towards black 6." In reality, the caller is simply telling the desk operator that he is static in one location, a cafe or a bar, for example.

MAKE YOUR OWN SPOT CODEBOOK

Get hold of a street map of your local area. Next, purchase a small sheet of coloured spot labels from your local stationery shop. Just stick the spots onto the map at each of the major intersections or streets. Next, number the spots. Depending on the number of people you intend to trust with your spot codebook, make a number of photocopies. It is a great way of staying in touch with your friends or meeting people at specific locations.

Creating Safe Spot Codes

Use the coloured spots for one area but make the numbers random. This will help confuse the enemy, yet it will make no difference to the agent.

Invisible Writing

Writing invisible messages is also a good way of passing information between people. Despite having been around for centuries, this technique is still widely used by many intelligence agencies today.

One of the problems with traditional invisible ink is that the author cannot see what they are writing. As a result, the message has to be short and very precisely written.

Then, some years ago, the British intelligence service discovered, purely by accident, that a Pentel Rollerball makes a brilliant tool for invisible writing. The rollerball writes normally on a piece of paper. The writing is then pressed against the piece of paper that will carry the secret message. The original ink dries almost immediately, so to the eye the message paper looks blank. However, when it is swabbed with a developing fluid, the message miraculously appears. It therefore allows the author to write a detailed and well-spaced letter in real time and transfer it to a blank piece of paper by what is known as "offset" printing. The transferred message will only become visible when it is developed.

MAKE YOUR OWN INVISIBLE INK

Any clear (not visible to the eye when dry), carbon-based liquid can be used to make invisible ink; milk and lemon juice being the most common. It is best to use normal writing or computer paper, as glossy and absorbent paper distorts the writing. Use an old-fashioned metal nib pen, although a toothpick would suffice. Dip this into the milk or lemon juice and simply write your letter. The wetness provides some idea of what you have written, but once the liquid is dry then it will disappear.

The best way to read your message is to use a domestic iron. Let the iron heat up and then rub it over the paper. Because the liquid is carbon-based, it will turn brown and thus develop your message. Agents have used various forms of heat, such as gently moving the paper over a candle flame, in order to reveal the hidden message.

Ingenious Codes

Some of the codes that have developed over the centuries have been truly ingenious and, while these are rarely used today, it is worth looking at them.

Although the best way of transcribing a message is to use the alphabet, the alphabetic and figure form can transcribe into symbols or sound blocks. While the best example of the latter is Morse code, many intelligence agencies have experimented with microwave and other sound devices.

ENCODING AND DECODER RINGS

This a very simple substitution cipher, but one that can be used over and over while changing the code each time. Basically you need two wheels, one that is about 1 cm smaller than the other. These wheels can be made of any material you can write on.

Around the outer edge of each wheel write the alphabet and the numbers 0 through to 9. It is best to use the clock-face method to ensure that your writing is evenly spaced, taking care that the outer and inner markings are directly in line with each other. The idea is that the smaller disk can rotate inside the larger.

STEP ONE

To encode a message, simply turn the inner disk to wherever you wish to start. For example: rotate the inner disk until the A is now aligned with P. Using the outer disk as your plain text write down the aligned letter on the inner disk to form your code. Be careful when matching the inner and outer circle, some letters have a wider base than others, if you are not sure count them off.

STEP TWO

It is a simple matter of passing the code to the handler or agent together with the original start place on the outer disk; in this instance P. You can complicate the matter by having a more complicated start code, P7–V4–S6. To decode the message, first place the inner disk at P and read off the first seven letters. The inner disk will then be moved to V for the next four letters and to S for the remaining six. Don't forget to keep your decoded message in blocks.

Creating Encoder & Decoder Rings

The best way to do this is to create two alphabetical and figure disks using Microsoft Word. Print them out and stick the paper on to cardboard to ensure a more secure platform. Pin them together in the middle so that the inner wheel rotates.

Computers

There is nothing new about computer encryption. It uses the same cryptography methods that have been used for centuries.

Few people, other than government intelligence agencies, had any need for cryptography prior to the digital age. That has all changed today. Businesses and individuals all generate information which, for one reason or another, they wish to remain secret. The difference in normal human forms of cryptology and those developed for computers is simply one of security, i.e. it is easy for a computer to crack a human code, but not visa versa. Most computer encryption systems belong in one of two categories – symmetric-key encryption and public-key encryption.

Symmetric-key encryption is a secret code based on one individual computer. In order for one computer to send the encrypted message to another computer, the second computer must first know the same secret code. The secret code is the key to unlocking the information.

Example: In a simple form, you send a text-encoded message to another computer telling the user that the secret code is 3. The encrypted process automatically changes the alphabetical information letters to 3 down i.e. A becomes D and B becomes E etc.

This is a very simple explanation of how computer encryption works, but it should be stated that today's encryption systems are highly advanced. Public-key encryption uses both a private key and a public key. Whereas only your computer knows the private key, any other computer that wants secure communications can access your computer's public key. In order to decode the incoming message, the receiving computer must have and use both the public and the private keys.

Simple Secret Data Transmission

One of the simplest ways to transmit secret data is to use the "Options" button found in the "Tools" file of Microsoft Word. Click on the "Security" box and you will be asked for a password. (For Mac users, go to the "Protect document" option in "Tools" and follow the same procedure.) You will next be asked to reconfirm your password. After which your document is secure not only on your computer, but even when you email it to someone else. They must first ask you for the secret password.

Hiding a Text File in a Digital Picture

One way of sending secret messages is to hide your confidential data in inconspicuous graphic files. This file is then sent to your friend over the Internet or on a disk. With the appropriate software and code word, the text can be taken out of the picture.

One such system uses the well-known steganography technology that is also used for digitally watermarking pictures. Bitmap graphics consist of pixels that can be modified to store your text. If the altered picture – containing your text file – is then seen by someone else, it will simply look like a normal image. It works by removing or altering some of bits that make up the picture pixels, and replacing them with your text. To the human eye these changes cannot be seen as only insignificant information is removed and this is done across the whole spectrum of the digital image.

3 SURVEILLANCE

There are many forms of surveillance but, for the most part, people believe that they can go about their everyday lives expecting a certain amount of privacy – this is not true. Every single person in Europe is under some form of surveillance every day. They will not deliberately be observed or overheard, but records of their movements and actions will be recorded. Close Circuit Television (CCTV) cameras currently monitor city centres, major stores, petrol stations and motorways. Credit card transactions can be traced. Your emails can be read, as can every stroke of the keyboard. And then there is Echelon...

Echelon

Echelon is the name given to the massive worldwide surveillance system that is capable of capturing and scanning every telephone call, fax and email sent anywhere in the world.

Using sophisticated satellite systems, earth stations, radar and communication networks, as well as an array of ships and planes, the system is capable of monitoring both military and civilian communications.

Although details about the system are still shrouded in secrecy, some facts are known. The main proponents are the US and the UK, but they are backed up by Canada, Australia and New Zealand. Each country is responsible for monitoring a certain part of the Earth. For example, the US listens in over most of Latin America, Asia, Asiatic Russia and northern China. Britain monitors Europe, Africa and Russia west of the Urals. Canada sweeps the northern parts of the former USSR and the Arctic regions. Australia is responsible for Indochina, Indonesia and southern China, whereas New Zealand handles the western Pacific.

In practice, the way Echelon works is simple. All the members of the alliance use satellites, ground receiving stations and electronic intercepts which enable them to pick up all communications traffic sent by satellite, cellular, microwave and fibre-optic means. The communications captured by these methods are then sent to a series of supercomputers that are programmed to recognize predetermined phrases, addresses, words or known voice patterns. Anything deemed to be of interest is then sent to the relevant intelligence agency for analysis. Following 9/11, it must be assumed that Echelon is on alert for any messages that might warn of an attack by Al Quaeda.

What is Surveillance?

Surveillance is a technique used to obtain information, to make connections, to produce new leads and to collate evidence. Surveillance can be carried out by one of the following methods.

- **Human, visual and audio.**
- **Electronic, video and audio.**
- **Aerial and satellite surveillance.**

Surveillance may be carried out in order to obtain evidence of a crime or to identify persons who have been indicated in subversive actions. Surveillance methods help establish a person's location, and may well lead to knowledge of an an association with other criminals. The location of stolen or contraband goods can be exposed, leading to an admissible case in court. However, the main way that surveillance is used is to gather military intelligence. Governments have long since learned that information gathered on the potential lethality and capabilities of another nation can help them prepare for defence or attack.

In reality, surveillance is simply monitoring the activity of a person or persons, a place or an object. In order to do this successfully, intelligence agents need to consider several factors about the target. For example, if the target is a person then he will most probably move around, either on foot or by vehicle. If the target is in a house in the country, a static observation position (OP) would be set up. The various methods of surveillance consist of one or a combination of the following:

- **Static surveillance.**
- **Foot surveillance.**
- **Mobile surveillance.**
- **Technical surveillance.**

Surveillance Operator

A good surveillance operator is known as a "grey" person. That is to say that they mingle with people, but that no one ever takes any notice of them.

Their personality appears nondescript, they have no outstanding physical features and their dress is innocuous. They are deliberately trained to be Mr. and Mrs. Nobody; so insignificant that no one ever gives them a second glance.

Yet this is only an outward appearance. The surveillance operator requires many skills. They must be patient, as surveillance operations can go on for months, sometimes even years. They must be adaptable, as many targets can act erratically. If the target is a professional spy, they will deliberately check to see if they are being followed and will take evasive actions in order to throw off any unseen surveillance operation being carried out against them.

Surveillance operators must have confidence not only in their own abilities but also in those of their team members. They must have a good memory, good hearing and excellent eyesight. Most of all, though, surveillance operators must blend into the background and become almost invisible. If the target takes a bus, one of the team must follow. The target will observe anyone who entered the bus at the same stop and be aware that they may be surveillance operators. In this situation, the surveillance operator becomes an actor, conversing with the passenger next to him as if they have known each other for years. The target may even approach the surveillance operator and deliberately confront him as to why they are being followed. In this instance, the operator must deliver a response that satisfies the target's inquisition.

The surveillance operator must also learn advanced driving skills and be able to operate any number of different vehicles. Most surveillance operators in the United Kingdom undertake a high-speed driving course with the police. This involves handling a vehicle at speed. They must also have a good knowledge of the area in which they are working. Above all, they must possess and develop a "sixth sense" – something that comes with good training and experience.

Some surveillance operators specialize in technical surveillance. They must learn how to use and operate a whole myriad of technical equipment, such as cameras and listening devices. In many cases this means covertly breaking into someone's property and inserting an audio-visual device. To do this successfully, surveillance operators are required to learn method of entry skills such as lock picking. Other operations may require them to crawl beneath a vehicle during the hours of darkness and insert a tracking device.

It is important for the surveillance operator to understand who or what the target is. If the target is a person, he needs to ask himself whether that person is aware that they may be under surveillance. If the target is a foreign spy, then he will have been trained in counter-surveillance methods. Even if the target is a common criminal, he may, due to the nature of his activities, become suspicious of being followed. In many cases, a surveillance target may not be aware that he is being watched or followed, or he may have been getting away with his activities for so long that he has become complacent. Knowing these factors helps the surveillance team decide on the number of people required and what approach they should take. Likewise, where the target is a static location, such as a building, it is important for the surveillance operators to evaluate what resources are needed.

Master of Disguise

There may be times when a spy or agent is required to become a master of disguise, and there are two basic methods: the immediate quick change and the deliberate disguise.

Even a quick change requires some thorough and prior preparation. For instance, it is possible to change your stature, dress or appearance or a combination of all three. Stature can be addressed by stooping, limping, effecting a height change or body bulk size. Changing your dress requires converting something you are already wearing or having an alternative item of clothing with you. Likewise your appearance can be changed in a few minutes if you are prepared. The basic rules are to start off as Mr. Average and change into Mr. Nondescript. The following pointers will help. That is to say it is easier to dress down than it is to dress up – by the same token it is easier to look older than it is to try and look younger. All these tricks can be done on the move, but they are best performed while temporary unsighted, such as in a crowded pub toilet. Changing you ethnic appearance is a good ploy to use at night or during foul weather. Here are a few suggestions:

- **Place a stone in your sock to create a realistic limp.**
- **Make yourself look taller by adding rigid foam pads to your shoes.**
- **Wear a cap. When you remove it, it makes you look shorter.**
- **Place half a folded newspaper on each shoulder to make your waist look thinner.**
- **Put cotton wool in your mouth to swell out your cheeks.**
- **Put on or remove glasses.**
- **Burn a cork and blacken your face where you normally shave to imitate stubble.**
- **Use soot, burnt paper, talcum powder or cigarette ash to change your hair colour.**
- **Carry items in your pockets to help create a different look such as a carry bag, fold-up walking stick, cigarettes, baseball cap or a plastic raincoat.**

A deliberate disguise is a more planned affair, but the same basic tactics apply. If your reason for disguise is to visit a place and not look out of place, it is always worth doing a recce of the area to pick up ideas. Never be inclined to dress so that you bring attention upon yourself. If the area is festooned with tourists, tramps or students dress accordingly.

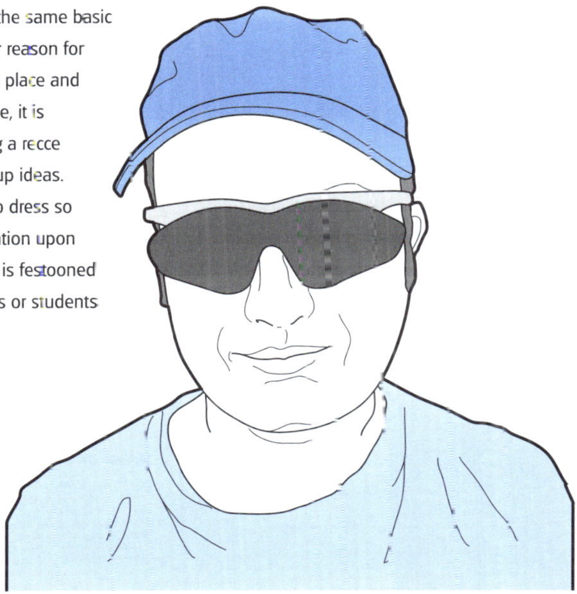

Surveillance Voice Procedure

Vehicle surveillance operators must learn some basic codes and a jargon that whilst being slick and brief, is also clear enough for all personnel to understand.

There are several reasons for doing this; firstly it helps identify who is doing what and where a particular surveillance vehicle is in relation to the others. Secondly, it helps minimize the amount of voice traffic over the radio.

One such code, popular with surveillance teams, is the phonetic alphabet. It can be used to identify targets, vehicles, operators and places. Numbers are added to enlarge and identify various units, for example, vehicle SP4 would be spoken as "Sierra Papa Four" and be part of a Special Patrol surveillance team.

The Phonetic Alphabet

A......Alpha	N......November
B......Bravo	O......Oscar
C......Charlie	P......Papa
D......Delta	Q......Quebec
E......Echo	R......Romeo
F......Foxtrot	S......Sierra
G......Golf	T......Tango
H......Hotel	U......Uniform
I......India	V......Victor
J......Juliet	W......Whisky
K......Kilo	X......X-ray
L......Lima	Y......Yankee
M......Mike	Z......Zulu

Surveillance operators also use other terminologies to indicate a number of actions the target vehicle is likely to carry out. This terminology also helps the surveillance team keep the target vehicle within sight and thus avoid a lost contact. While they vary from country to country, here are a few examples of common vehicle surveillance terminology with an explanation as to what each means.

TYPICAL TERMINOLOGY USED BY VEHICLE SURVEILLANCE TEAMS

"Back-up, can you?"	Eyeball request to back-up vehicle to ascertain whether a handover is appropriate. Response is either "Yes, yes", "No, no" or "Back-up can at next junction".
Back-up	The second vehicle in the convoy.
Cancel	Ignore the instruction or information just given.
"Come through."	Given after "hang back" to bring the convoy through.
"Committed."	The target vehicle is committed to traveling on the motorway.
"Contact, contact."	The eyeball has been regained by one of the vehicles in the convoy, following the search procedure. The pick-up vehicle will also give a location.
"Convoy check."	Request from eyeball to determine position of vehicles in convoy, to which all vehicles automatically respond in turn. Motorcyclists should respond without specifying their precise position, after Tail-End Charlie has reported. When all correct, eyeball calls "convoy complete".
"Down to you."	The final transmission made by eyeball before handing over surveillance to another vehicle.
"Eyeball regained."	The target vehicle is once more under surveillance.
Eyeball.	The vehicle or officer that has primary visual contact with the target and that is directing the operation for the time being.
"Footman out."	A vehicle in the convoy has put an officer out on foot.
"Going round."	The target vehicle is commencing a second or subsequent circuit of the roundabout.
"Hang back."	Transmission from eyeball, indicating that the convoy should hold back as the target is slowing down or has stopped.

"Held.	The target has made a temporary stop. This will normally be followed by an explanation for the stop, ie. traffic lights, pedestrian crossing, traffic congestion etc.
"Left, left, left."	The target vehicle has turned left. In some cases, such as on a motorway, the junction number may be added, i.e. "left, left, left 57".
"Manoeuvering."	Warning issued by eyeball, indicating that target is, for example, manoeuvering on the forecourt of a garage, business premises, car park etc.
Nearside, offside.	Indicates that the nearside/offside traffic indicator is active on the target vehicle.
"No change."	The situation remains unaltered.
"No deviation."	The target vehicle is continuing straight ahead, as at a crossroads. It is said to reassure the team that there has been no change of direction.
"Not one, not two."	The target vehicle negotiating a roundabout has passed first, second exits etc.
"Off, off, off."	Transmission by the eyeball, indicating that the target is now on the move.
"Original, original."	The target has resumed after a stop, in the same direction of travel as before.
"Out, out, out."	Transmission by the eyeball, indicating that the target is alighting from a vehicle or that he is leaving a premises.
"Reciprocal, reciprocal."	The target vehicle has done a U-turn and is now returning along the same route.
"Right, right, right."	The target vehicle has turned right.
"Roundabout"	The target is approaching a traffic roundabout where he has a multiple choice of exit.
"Roger, so far?"	An intermittent request by the transmitting officer asking recipients whether they have understood a lengthy period of dialogue.
Shadow car.	The vehicle being used to support the footman.
"Stand down."	Cancellation of whole operation.
"Standby, standby."	Instruction issued by eyeball, alerting convoy to possible movement of target.

"Stop, stop, stop."	Target vehicle has stopped in circumstances other than a "held" situation; the target vehicle is slowing down and may be about to stop; or conditions require caution.
Tail-End Charlie.	The vehicle at the rear of the convoy.
"Taken first/second."	The target vehicle has taken the first, the second exit etc.
Target.	The person who is the target of the observation.
"Loss of eyeball."	A temporary visual loss of the target vehicle has occurred.
Total loss.	The eyeball has not been regained after the temporary loss. A total loss will normally be followed by a pre-planned search procedure.
"We are bulked."	Only the target can be held.
"Who has?"	Used to confirm the surveillance vehicle with the current eyeball on the target.
"Who's backing?"	Request from eyeball vehicle to confirm there is a back-up vehicle ready to take over.

Note: Certain surveillance units, such as the British SAS, would not include "Contact, contact" in their surveillance voice procedure as this code word is reserved purely to indicate physical contact, i.e. they are engaged in a firefight.

Assuming that we have a basic three-vehicle surveillance team Sierra One, Two and Three, with Sierra One having eyeball and with the team using a simple spot code system, a typical conversation might go as follows:

"All stations this is Sierra One – I have eyeball – towards green 25. Who's backing?"

"Sierra Three – backing." (Indicating that they are behind Sierra One.)

"Sierra Two – Roger that." (Sierra two confirming situation awareness.)

"Sierra One – target still straight 50/60." (Indicating that the target is continuing at a straight speed of 50–60 mph.)

"Sierra Two – Roger that." (Confirmation.)

"Sierra Three – Roger that." (Confirmation.)

"Left, left, left – Sierra Two can you?" (The target vehicle has turned left and Sierra One is asking Sierra Two if they can take the eyeball position.)

"That's a roger." (Sierra Two confirms that they will take up the eyeball.)

"Sierra Three – Backing." (Confirming that Sierra Three has moved into the backing position.)

You will note that the voice procedure becomes clipped as the unit progresses into the follow. Familiarity and good co-operation between surveillance operators all help minimize the airtime, but will still provide everyone with a verbal picture of what is happening.

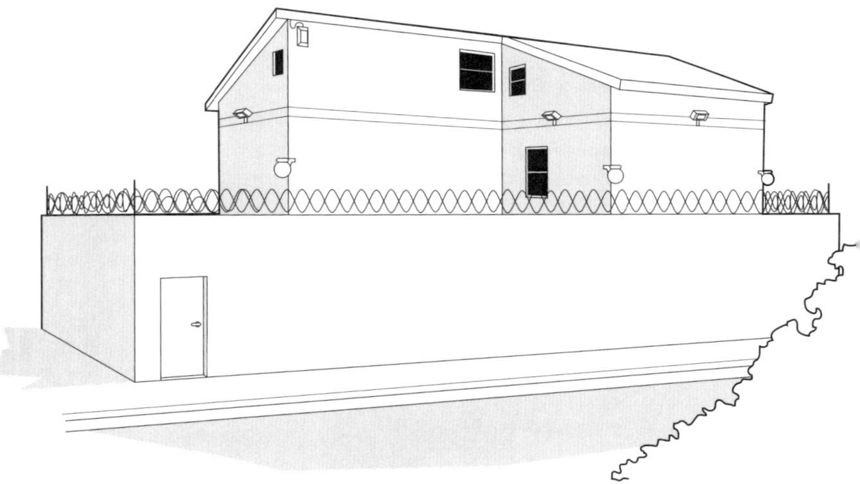

Garbology

Garbology simply means taking the trash or garbage from a household or business and examining it. It can prove a very good source of information, providing confirmation and relevant details about a target.

The idea is to collect a target's garbage discreetly and to examine it at leisure, recording all of the items that it contains. The main advantage of garbology is that it is both non-obtrusive and that it almost always goes unnoticed – another advantage is that it is legal in most countries.

GARBOLOGY TECHNIQUES

Once your target is housed, make a note of the garbage disposal system. These may vary from town to town and from country to country, but in almost all cases, the garbage is picked up by a waste disposal company. Watch and make a note of the garbage truck's date and time of arrival at the target premises. Check to see if the garbage container is for an individual use or for many houses. In many countries, the individual must take their garbage to a shared container. If this is the case, you must establish whether the target takes out his garbage at certain times.

Watch and observe the best time to collect the target's garbage. The hours of darkness are best, but if a pick-up has to be made during daylight hours, dress accordingly, in the manner of a down and out, carrying a plastic bag, for example. Always remember to wear a pair of rubber gloves, as some bins can be very unhygienic.

Lay out the garbage contents on a large plastic sheet and discard all useless items such a food waste. Always keep a written note as to the type of food being consumed, i.e. fast food, expensive food etc. Next, check each individual item and make notes on each. For example:

- **Count the number of cigarettes butts and identify the brand.**
- **Count the number of alcohol bottles or cans and identify the make.**
- **Set aside all correspondence, including papers such as telephone bills, bank statements, for detailed examination later.**
- **Photograph any items that may be of interest, such as discarded clothing, magazines, computer disks or empty non-food packaging.**

- **Carry out an in-depth examination of all correspondence and paper products.**
- **Write down your observations and conclusions for each separate garbage pick-up.**
- **You should carry out at least four separate pick-ups within the period of a month in order to make a minimum assessment.**
- **Report any important discoveries that you think may be of immediate interest and use to the current operation.**

Protect Yourself

Never throw anything away that could prove your identity or that could provide important information to others. Buy a steel bucket and make a "burn bin". Simply burn all of your unsolicited mail and unwanted bank statements before disposal. Only put discarded food in the bin. If you think you are being watched, discreetly place your garbage back in someone else's bin. Never throw away any statements which have address correction slips attached, as a person can request for a new card to be sent to a different address, and they may already have your signature from discarded credit card receipts.

Clothesline Assessment

When you are in a position to observe a target's house, don't forget to look at the clothesline. Almost all households, including flats, hang out some washing during the week, sometimes on the same day every week. Observing the clothesline over a period of a month can provide the following information: the number of people living at the address, their rough age and their sex.

The outcome from a good garbology probe over several weeks can be very revealing. The information gathered should be properly documented with a list of attributes added to the target's file. Here are some of the things you might expect to find out about the target:

- **His correct name and address.**
- **His personal finances, including the name of his bank and his account number.**
- **His credit card usage.**
- **His signature. (Taken from discarded credit card receipts.)**
- **The telephone numbers he may dial, especially repetitive numbers**
- **His email address.**
- **His work or employment address.**
- **The amount of cigarettes he smokes.**
- **The amount of alcohol he consumes.**
- **Toiletries that he uses.**
- **A rough idea of his weekly expenditure.**

The list of clear and precise information that can be obtained through garbology is endless, but it needs to be done in a methodical way and there are some important things to consider. One factor to take into account is the number of people being catered for at the target's premises. If the target lives alone this is not a problem. One quick way of determining household numbers is to carry out a clothesline assessment.

Static Surveillance Outline

A static surveillance position is normally known as an "observation position" (OP), which can either be in an urban or a rural area. They are set up to observe a fixed location or object for a predetermined amount of time.

Their objective is to obtain information through the use of human visual and technical recording devices. Setting up an urban surveillance is quite difficult and depends largely on the selection of a safe location in which to install the OP. Where possible, the urban OP should have the best vantage point from which to observe the target building. This will include both the entry and exit points of the building, something that is crucial to establish both the movements of the target and any other visitors that he may have.

RURAL OP

An OP is a covert site from where surveillance activities can be carried out and intelligence gathered. Field agents are experts in setting up OPs and remaining in them for long stretches. The secret of a good rural OP is to make sure that it blends in with the natural surroundings.

Wherever an OP is located, the rules for its construction remain the same. A site must not be vulnerable to discovery and must afford a good view of the target position. A concealed entrance and exit are also needed. Once the site has been chosen, the OP should be constructed under cover of night. If this is not possible, then some natural daytime cover should be invented – road works for example. The structure can be made out of any material as long as the end product blends in with everything around it and cannot be easily seen.

In addition to food, water and sleeping bags, operational gear is also stored inside the OP: weapons, radio equipment, binoculars, cameras and telescopes. This can make conditions uncomfortable. No sign of the spies' presence can be lef as it might mean the OP is discovered. Therefore, even private functions, such as urinating and defecating must be done in the OP.

URBAN OP

The Urban OP is situated in a populated area, which means it is in some type of building. The final location is normally a room overlooking the target house; observation equipment is installed in such a way as to monitor the target, while remaining undetected from the outside. The room, or adjoining rooms, should be prepared to accommodate the surveillance operators on duty.

Likewise, the entrance to the OP from the street should be from the rear if possible. Most major cites are crammed with civilians, some of whom are curious. As a result, a logical explanation should be prepared to explain the occupation of the OP when it is surrounded by other residents. Here are a few considerations for setting up an urban OP.

- **Location must have good visual access over the target location.**
- **Good radio communications to the control desk and the foot and mobile units are vital.**
- **Correct surveillance equipment, cameras, telescopes etc, need to be installed.**
- **Entry to and from the OP should be covert in nature.**
- **The OP needs to be large enough to accommodate at least two operators.**
- **The OP needs to have cooking and toilet facilities.**
- **Unobtrusive changeover routines need to be set up.**

In essence, a good urban OP is a room from which you can observe the target and record his movements without being detected. In some cases, the intelligence agency may put an OP in an occupied house. If the position is the best one available, then a thorough check will be made on the occupants before they are approached. Even then, occupants are given a cover story, i.e. the operators are from the "drugs squad" and have a suspect under surveillance.

Foot Surveillance Techniques

In general, targets are not followed once, but many times. In doing so, the surveillance operators build up a pattern of the target's general behaviour.

If this is the case, surveillance will be termed as "loose" and the operators will remain at a safe distance to avoid being compromised. Surveillance on the target can be done in short stages until a number of known "triggers" can be identified i.e. at 5:05 pm from Monday to Friday they leave their place of employment. Loose surveillance is normally carried out against a target who is living in a fixed location for a given period of time.

If the target has recently arrived in the country, or has suddenly come to the attention of the intelligence services, then the initial surveillance will be "close". This means having the target visual at all times during the surveillance. This form of surveillance requires the very best operators and their aim is to establish some basic information about the target, such as housing, his employment and his associates. Once these basics are known, loose surveillance techniques can then be employed.

Both foot and mobile surveillance operations have three distinct phases: the trigger, or pick-up, the follow and the housing. Any operation will be based on the fact that you need a starting place, normally a location where you know the target to be, or where he will be going. The surveillance will involve following the identified target and, finally, placing them in a known abode, the target house, for example.

Trigger or Pick-up

If the target has not been located there can be no follow. It is vital, therefore, to have a good trigger. The type of trigger used can be static (best), mobile or technical.

If the target's house or place of employment is under constant observation by a static OP then this can be used to provide the trigger. The time that the operation commences will be deduced from static OP's events log. Surveillance units will be in position in good time and wait for the "standby" trigger from the static OP when they detect signs of target movement.

Where the target is in a difficult location, such as a large car park, the trigger may well come from vehicle surveillance operators covering either the target vehicle or the exits. Such instances can easily lead to a lost contact. This can be avoided by knowing the target's route and by positioning a second trigger vehicle at a critical location.

Both static and mobile triggers can be enhanced by the use of technical surveillance devices (see Tracking). These can be covertly fitted to the target vehicle either on a temporary or on a permanent basis. Most modern devices are generally at rest if a vehicle has been stationary for more than 15 minutes, and are then activated by the door opening and the key being turned in the ignition. The technical tracking device sends a very accurate position signal on demand from the desk operator; this can either be constant or at predetermined time intervals. The signal is displayed on a computer screen that has a street map overlay. The target's vehicle position can also be monitored with the use of small mobile phones used by the foot or vehicle surveillance operators. Other technical triggers, such as hidden microphones and cameras close to the targets premises, can also be used, but these are not as reliable as tracking systems, as these continue to be of use during the follow.

Once the trigger has been activated, in the case of a foot follow, the trigger will simply state the target is "foxtrot", or "mobile" with vehicle surveillance. The surveillance will commence until the team leader has decided that the target is "housed", at which time the operation is called off.

Single Person Surveillance

It is difficult for one person to conduct good foot surveillance, as by its very nature it means keeping the target visual at all times, but,as the saying goes, "If you can see him he can see you."

No matter how good the individual, if he is following someone who has been trained in counter-surveillance techniques, the chances are he will be compromised. However, there are opportune times, such as when a suspect target is inadvertently recognized by an off-duty surveillance operator. As odd at it might sound, in many large cities, off-duty surveillance operators have entered a restaurant, stepped on to a bus or have been driving along in traffic, when they have recognized a known target. At this juncture, the target is usually unaware of the chance sighting and is happily going about his business – for the surveillance operator it is an ideal opportunity.

While the follow may only be brief, there is a chance that it could provide some interesting information. The key to successful single person surveillance is not to remain too close, but to choose a good vantage position, such as a corner on a street junction, which allows you to observe four streets at the same time. For a surveillance operator acting alone, or when close surveillance is employed, there are a few basic rules.

- **If opportune target is acquired – call for back-up.**
- **When in a congested area, close up on the target**
- **In less congested areas, hang back and stay loose.**
- **Take out your shopping bag and look into the shop windows.**
- **Assess the target's walk speed, impetus and activity i.e. are they shopping, going for a social drink etc?**
- **Observe target's alertness and note any counter-surveillance activity.**

DETECTING COUNTER-SURVEILLANCE

It is important for the surveillance operators to recognize signs of counter-surveillance. This helps identify whether the target is actively engaged in unlawful activities or whether he is simply displaying normal social behaviour. A known target that is about to meet his handler or agent will almost certainly carry out some counter-surveillance techniques. When doing so, the target will watch to see who reacts unnaturally or who is taken by surprise. He will observe any person who suddenly changes direction or looks to be giving a signal to another person. These are just a few of the signs that he would be looking for:

- **Stopping, turning and looking at anyone to their rear.**
- **Making a sudden change of direction or reversing their course.**
- **Walking slowly and then speeding up suddenly.**
- **Turning a corner and stopping to see who comes round it.**
- **Walking round the block.**
- **Going into a building, such as a pub, and immediately exiting via another door.**
- **Checking constantly in the reflection of a shop window.**
- **Waiting to the last minute to step on to a bus or an underground train.**
- **Getting off at the next stop, waiting and catching the next bus or train.**
- **Deliberately dropping something to see if anyone picks it up.**
- **Changing their appearance or clothing.**

Foot Surveillance Team

The basic surveillance foot team consists of a three-person unit. The unit's main objective is to keep at least two sets of eyeballs on the target at all times. The basic procedure for keeping a target under observation is as follows:

- **STAGE ONE – on target trigger, the first operator will remain behind the target.**
- **The second operator hangs back to keep the first operator in view.**
- **The third operator will walk on the opposite side of the street, almost parallel with the target.**
- **STAGE TWO – on a linear follow, one and two may change places as and when necessary. If the target changes to the other side of the street, number three takes up the immediate follow, with number two moving across the street as back-up. Number one will remain parallel to the target.**
- **STAGE THREE – on target turning left or right. Number one operator will go straight across the road and take up parallel position. Number two can choose to take up the lead while number three crosses the road to become back-up.**
- **If the target is deemed to be of particular importance, then several foot surveillance teams will be deployed at the same time. It is possible during the follow for a target to adopt a mode of transport. For this reason, most surveillance is a combination of both foot and mobile.**

- **If the target enters a telephone booth, number one should walk past and take up a location in front of the target. Number two should enter the adjacent booth, if there is one, enter money and make a real call, back to the office for example. Discreetly try to observe any actions the target makes and listen to his conversation if possible.**
- **Never enter a phone box while carrying a mobile phone, as this is a dead giveaway.**
- **If the target drops an item, it should be collected. Be aware, however, that this could also be a ploy on behalf of the target to see if he is being followed.**
- **Always make a note of any person the target gives anything to. While the purchase of a newspaper may seem innocent it is also a perfect way of passing a message.**

STAGE ONE

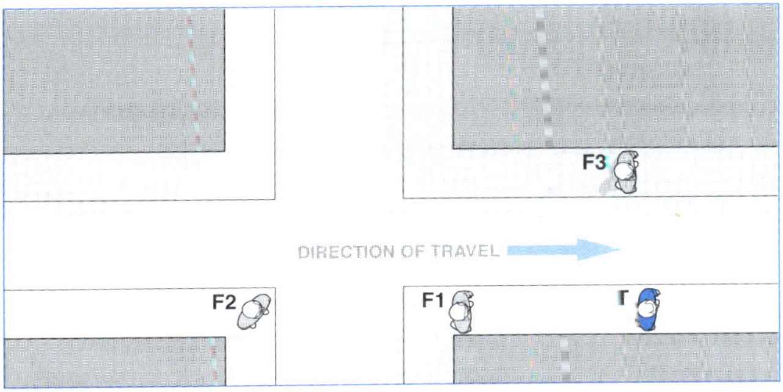

STAGE TWO

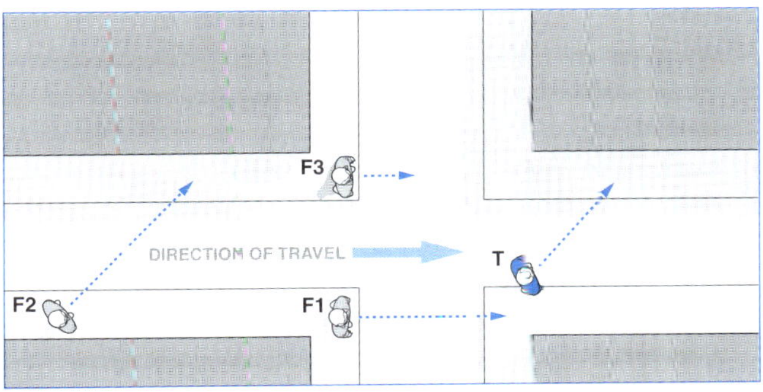

STAGE THREE

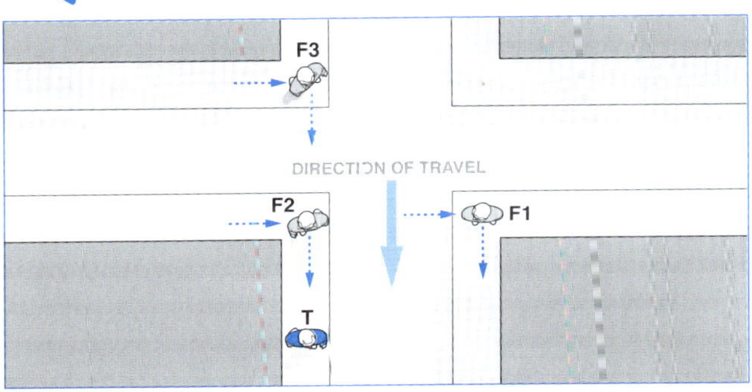

Recording Information

It is not enough simply to follow the target around to see where he goes. A detailed report must be kept.

One of the primary reasons for people becoming spies or agents is monetary reward. Foot surveillance provides the opportunity to see how much money a person is spending each month. How much does he spend in the supermarket, the pub or on new items, such as televisions and other electrical goods? The monthly total can be easily checked against the target's normal earnings. Several targets have been caught out in this way. Here are some pointers to watch out for:

- **Does the target lead a lavish lifestyle compared to his known income?**
- **What type of credit card is the target using? Does he use the same cashpoint on a regular basis?**
- **Does the target have any sexual preferences? Does he visit gay bars or prostitutes etc?**
- **How much alcohol does the target consume?**
- **Does the target compromise himself, i.e. has he been seen with a rent boy?**
- **Is the target a user of drugs?**
- **Where does the target visit frequently?**
- **Are there any unusual deviations in an otherwise normal route to and from a location?**
- **Does the target employ counter-surveillance tactics?**

The answers to these questions and many more provide the surveillance team with vital information. If the target is a gay, drug-taking type who likes to throw his money around, the intelligence agency may well find him a lover. Visits to the same location, on a regular basis, may indicate a DLB. If the information is extremely good it may be used to confront the agent and turn them into a double agent.

Mobile Surveillance Outline

Mobile surveillance involves the use of vehicles, boats or aircraft to follow a target that is also mobile in some mode of transport.

This type of surveillance requires skilful driving, good observation, set procedures and excellent communications. It also takes a lot of discipline on behalf of the driver, as surveillance more than often turns into a chase rather than a discreet follow.

The same basic principles that apply to foot surveillance also apply to vehicle surveillance. However, the basic principles of vehicle surveillance are more difficult because of the complications created by traffic congestion, restrictions imposed by traffic laws and the increased possibility of the operation being discovered. Just as is the case with foot surveillance, an individual operating in a single vehicle will be limited in his capability, whereas a team of vehicles acting together will enhance the prospects of a successful operation.

The surveillance vehicle should accommodate either two or three people, thus making a foot follow possible in the event of a target going foxtrot. Having at least two people in the vehicle will also allow the driver to concentrate on his driving while the passenger remains alert to the surroundings.

A driver can use numerous techniques to reduce the risk of detection, such as switching off one of the headlights during a night-time follow. This will confuse the target if he is watching in his rear-view mirror. To make the target's car more easily recognizable, a distinctive feature could be attributed to it, such as smashing the tail-light. To make this look natural, always do it when the vehicle is parked in a busy street or in a car park. Also be aware that this may tip the target off to the surveillance operation.

When the target vehicle is temporarily parked, one of the surveillance operators should go on foot while the other remains with the vehicle. If the target vehicle is parked for any length of time, the surveillance vehicles should intermittently move their position. Those remaining in the car should also sit in the passenger seat to make it appear as though they are waiting for someone.

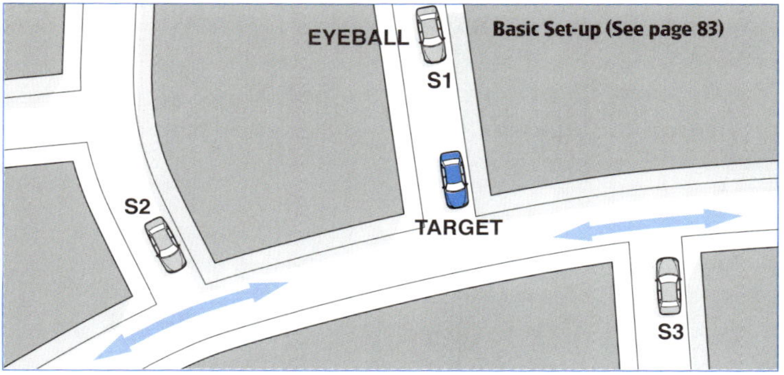
Basic Set-up (See page 83)
EYEBALL
S1
TARGET
S2
S3

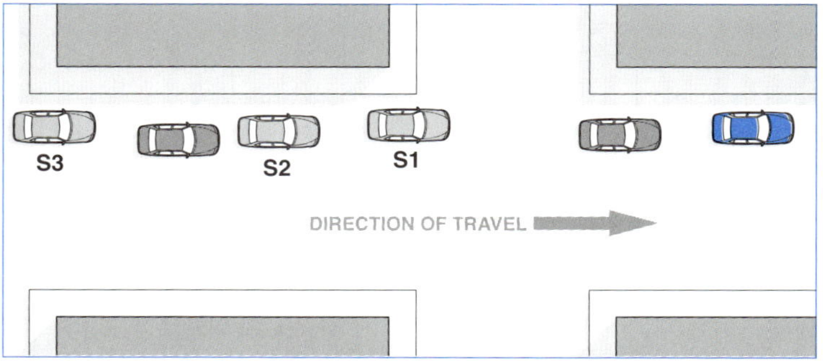
S3
S2
S1
DIRECTION OF TRAVEL

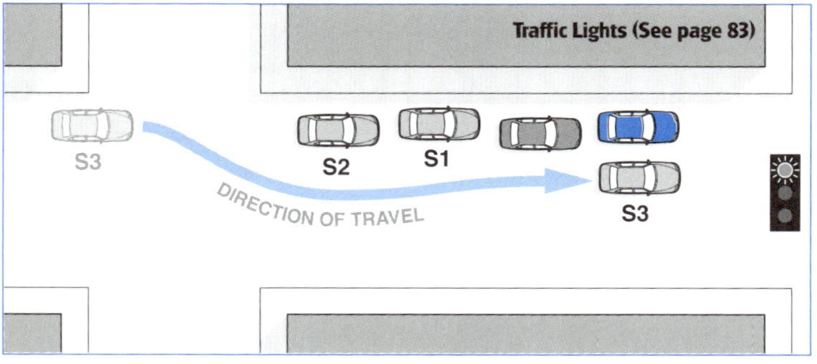
Traffic Lights (See page 83)
S3
S2
S1
DIRECTION OF TRAVEL
S3

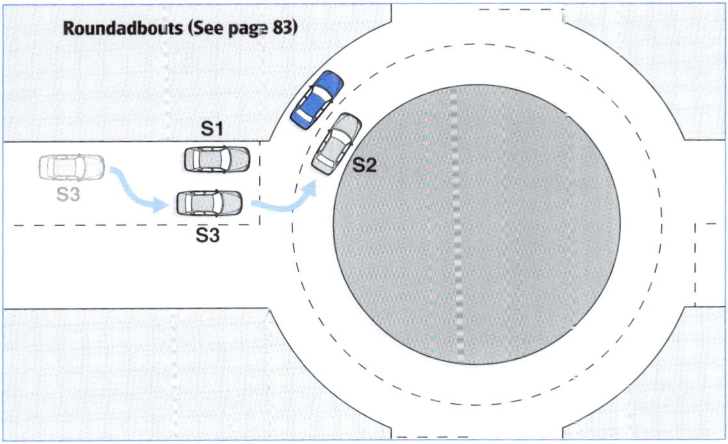

Roundadbouts (See page 83)

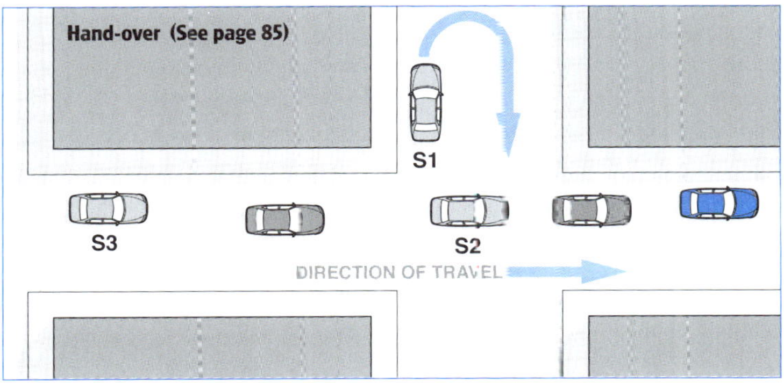

Hand-over (See page 85)

Good area knowledge will avoid the need to constantly study the map, which means taking your eyes off the target. However, the introduction of onboard GPS tracking devices has alleviated this problem to some degree. Before any surveillance operation can begin, though, certain questions must be asked.

- **Is mobile surveillance the best way of achieving your goal?**
- **Is the operational area well known?**
- **Is the operational area urban or rural, i.e. will foot surveillance be required?**
- **Is the target's awareness level known?**
- **Is the target's vehicle known?**
- **What is the pick-up point or trigger?**

The answer to these questions is normally self-evident. If the target is likely to travel large distances, it may be better to employ a helicopter than to deploy six mobile surveillance vehicles. Likewise, the target may use a form of transport that can outrun or outmanoeuvre the surveillance vehicles, a motorbike, for example.

Knowing the trigger for the target vehicle is also vital. In the normal course of events, all team vehicles will familiarize themselves with the streets around the trigger. A briefing is given before the operation begins, at which point all surveillance vehicles will be given their call signs, assigned start points and time in position (known as the "plot up"). Once on the ground, one vehicle may decide to do a drive past or may decide to put an operator on foot in order to confirm the target's location, i.e. are the house lights on? Is the target's vehicle parked outside? The pattern of the vehicles will be set in such a way that they will trigger a follow, irrespective of which direction the target vehicle drives. As is the case with foot surveillance, the actual trigger will come from either a static OP, a foot operator or one of the surveillance vehicles. Communications are tested and all vehicles confirm "in position".

SURVEILLANCE VEHICLES

Surveillance vehicles come in all shapes and sizes. Each is designed to cover a different aspect of surveillance; they include static vehicles, mobile and airborne. The static vehicles are normally vans, but they can be cars or even lorries. Their main function is to monitor a target by parking up close to the target's dwelling or place of employment. Some are manned while others are left unmanned, but all are capable of listening, videoing or triggering the start of a surveillance follow.

Mobile Surveillance Vehicle

A vehicle selected for surveillance work must be mechanically sound, fitted for use in all weather conditions and suitable for the area in which the surveillance is to take place.

The vehicle should be a soft, non-descript colour such as grey, and it should not have any distinguishing marks, such as front-mirror-hanging dice or rear-window adverts. The surveillance vehicle pool should be large enough to allow the vehicles to be rotated on a regular basis.

Most surveillance vehicles incorporate many features as standard, such as the use of cut-off switches to activate or deactivate the headlights or brake lights. These are of particular importance when the vehicle is being used for a night-time drop-off or pick-up. In such instances, the driver will deactivate the brake light so as to give no indication that he is slowing down.

Covert radio systems are fitted as standard and are normally invisible to the untrained eye. The radio unit will be hidden within the car while the aerial will be formed into an induction loop and hidden under the roof lining. A presser switch will also be hidden under the carpet, normally near to the driver's or the passenger's hand or foot. Both driver and passengers will have a small hearing aid that picks up the incoming signal from the induction loop. A hidden microphone will transmit when they press the hidden hand or foot switch. Cameras, both fixed and video, can be added to the surveillance car, as can GPS navigation and other tracking devices.

The outer make and type of the vehicle can be deceptive. The rear boot may indicate a model with a 1300 cc engine, while in reality the car will have been modified to take a much larger capacity engine. Other modifications could include a powerful battery and improved radiator system to avoid overheating in long traffic delays.

Mobile Surveillance Techniques

Once intelligence officers have plotted up and it has been established that everyone is in position, it is simply a matter of waiting for the trigger that will action the surveillance. The pick-up phase will depend on the location and the amount of possible routes the target can take, an example is shown below.

Once the target indicates that he is about to move, the trigger gives the "standby". All vehicles will follow the procedure to acknowledge this by calling off their call sign in alphabetical order, i.e. Sierra One – Roger; Sierra Two – Roger, and so on. The drivers will then turn on their ignition, while everyone listens to the trigger commentary. This will be a step-by-step talk through.

"Target leaving house, locking door, heading for target vehicle, vehicle door open, ignition – target is mobile – Sierra Three can you?"

This indicates that the target has left his house, has got into his car and has driven off. The trigger will have established that the best-placed surveillance vehicle to eyeball the target is Sierra Three, and by simply asking confirms to everyone who is immediately behind the target. This is a difficult part of surveillance and it is vital that everyone knows what is happening and who is where. At this stage, it is vital that all surveillance vehicles fall into place, adopting their correct positions. However, it is also important that no one overreacts until the trigger has confirmed that the target is mobile – he may well leave the house and walk down the street. In such incidents, the trigger would simply end his message with the words "target is foxtrot". At which stage, if deemed necessary, foot surveillance would be employed.

Even the best plot-up positions can go wrong. Other road users can pull out in front of you at a critical moment for example, but the surveillance operator must remain calm and report the fact that the target is "unsighted". A good plot-up plan will cover all possible "choke points", leaving little to chance. However, in the event that the target is unsighted by everyone, the eyeball is up for grabs.

Surveillance Fleet

Assuming that one vehicle has taken up the eyeball, the others should fall into place, one immediately behind and one hanging back.

BASIC SET-UP

While the eyeball can be immediately behind the target, it is often better to have at least a one-car separation; the same applies to the back-up vehicle and tail end Charlie. If more than one set of surveillance vehicles are being deployed, they are usually kept running parallel to or in front of the target. The control desk should have a master map plotting who is where and advising on their best positions. Unlike the immediate surveillance team, these vehicles are not restricted to the target's speed and can manoeuvre into position more quickly to prepare themselves for a handover, should it prove necessary.

Unfortunately, mobile surveillance is hampered by a whole range of problems: road works, traffic lights, pedestrian crossings, accidents and roundabouts, to mention just a few. These are all possible places where the target can become unsighted. To some degree, these problems can be overcome if the eyeball or the desk operator gives sufficient notice. "Approaching roundabout" or "stopped at T-junction" are two examples.

TRAFFIC LIGHTS

If the follow is linear and spread out over several hundred yards, there is a possibility that the back-up vehicles will be stopped by traffic lights, while the target and eyeball pass through. Providing there are several lanes, all vehicles behind the target should change lanes and accelerate slightly towards the lights. While this may put them temporarily closer to the target, it also provides them with a better chance of staying in the follow. A similar system can be used to bracket the target vehicle wherever the road has multi-lanes.

ROUNDABOUTS

The surveillance fleet is also required to close up whenever the target vehicle is approaching a roundabout. This enables the follow to continue smoothly, regardless of the exit the target takes. The main problem comes when there is a build-up of traffic at major or busy roundabouts; this means that the target vehicle can pull ahead, while all the surveillance teams are held. In such a situation, the target may take any exit and thus become unsighted or lost altogether.

If the entry onto the roundabout is multi-lane, the back-up vehicles should close up, even if this means going parallel to the target. The idea is to enter the roundabout just after or at the same time as the target vehicle. This may require either back-up or tail-end Charlie doing a circuit of the roundabout, but they should be able to trigger which exit the target took. Commentary for approaching a roundabout should go something like this (Sierra 1 has the eyeball).

"Approaching blue 5." (Spot code indicating a roundabout.)
"Held at blue 5."
"Sierra Two – moving up."
"Sierra Three – moving up."
"On blue 5."
"Taken 1, 2 or 3." (Normally repeated and indicating the exit off the roundabout.)

SPEED

Speed and distance are very important during any surveillance follow. Driving at speed down small country lanes only causes attention. There are times, such as when the cars running parallel need to get into a forward position, where speeding is required, but this should only ever be done out of the target's vision. The best way to control speed is by the eyeball vehicle calling off the target's speed "still straight – 35/40". This should be enough to regulate all vehicles that are blind to the target. Never turn a follow into a high-speed chase.

MOTORWAYS

If the target takes the motorway, it usually suggests that the follow will cover a greater distance. One of the advantages of doing surveillance on a motorway is the fact that the traffic is all going one way. This allows the surveillance team to spread out and to hang back a lot more. It also means that the eyeball can stay in position for a longer period of time.

Motorways also provide the opportunity for pre-planning; that is to say, the target vehicle is restricted to certain movements. He can only get off the motorway at exits and stop, unless he breaks down, at service stations. This allows the surveillance team to pre-position vehicles ahead of the target. In both cases, advance warnings are clearly given by the motorway signs.

HAND-OVER

Hand-over of the eyeball can happen for numerous reasons. For example, if Sierra One is held coming onto the roundabout, they may well ask, "who can?" At this stage, the best-placed vehicle will take up the eyeball and indicate the fact: "Sierra Two – I have the eyeball." A hand-over can be affected any time there is a need to change the vehicle immediately behind the target. This cuts down the risk of compromise. Likewise surveillance teams may hand over the target to one another in order to place a new set of vehicles in the target's rear-view mirror. This is particularly important when doing surveillance in the countryside.

Hand-over should always take place whenever the eyeball has been in position for a long period of time. During the normal course of events, he will check to see if the back-up vehicle is ready to take over; "Back-up can you?" If the response is affirmative, the eyeball will indicate when.

At the same time, back-up will move up closer, but will make sure that he is discreet about his movement. There are many good and logical places where the eyeball can be handed over: junctions, lay-bys and garage forecourts being prime examples. Once a hand-over has been executed, all vehicles will acknowledge their new positions, i.e. back-up becomes eyeball, tail end Charlie becomes back-up and the original eyeball becomes tail end Charlie.

TARGET STOPPING

At some stage during the follow, the target vehicle will stop. This could be for any number of reasons: to fill up with petrol, to take a break, or simply because he has reached his destination. Whatever the reason, it is up to the eyeball to make the call, "Stop, stop, near side." The warning should be given in time to stop all cars in the rear, while the eyeball continues on past the target vehicle.

This may be a temporary halt, which will be indicated by the nature of the stop, i.e. if the target drives into a garage forecourt, or drives into a supermarket car park, it is most likely temporary. In the case of the latter, it will be up to the team leader to indicate if some of the operators should follow on foot. Details such as this will have been discussed during the initial briefing for the operation. While stopping at a garage most vehicles can be held until the target is known to be on the move once more. However, if the target moves into a larger area, such as a supermarket which will require foot surveillance, new plot-up positions will be assigned, together with a new trigger. This allows for a clean start whenever the target decides to move on once more.

NIGHT DRIVING

Night surveillance is difficult, especially in poor weather conditions. This means that the eyeball is required to get closer to the target vehicle and that frequent hand-overs have to take place. If you are checking your map or GPS, make sure that you do it with a small flexi-light and not with the car interior lights. It is best to remove the interior light altogether, especially if the operation is likely to require a lot of footwork and getting in and out of the car. The target will be able to spot these intermittent illuminations in his rear-view mirror. Also make sure that all the surveillance vehicles have working head, side and tail-lights, as a broken one is nothing more than a marker to the target.

If the back-up vehicle or tail end Charlie fall too far back, they may request the eyeball to "touch red". This is a request for eyeball to hit his brake lights for a few seconds, so that the others can re-establish position.

MOTORBIKE

Motorbikes are particularly well suited to mobile surveillance in heavy traffic. Their size, speed and manoeuvrability are far greater than a car. However, a motorbike is distinctive amid traffic and the rider needs to be highly trained. A motorbike is particularly good at searching ahead if the eyeball has been held up and has lost contact with the target. The bike can remain in contact with the target until the surveillance team can re-establish the eyeball. In many cases, the motorbike rider will act independently from the rest of the surveillance team, listening in to the follow conversation, while using his own initiative with regards to positioning. Motorbikes can perform several other functions during any mobile surveillance, such as picking up foot operators who have been left behind during a temporary stop.

Cat's Eyes

A target recce may be carried out as part of a surveillance operation. Once the operator has finished, he will require a pick-up. In the city, this can be arranged by simply stating a street or a location such as a pub. In the countryside, however, such places are hard to specify. If a surveillance operator wishes to be picked up at an unspecified location, he will simply use a set of "cat's eyes", so-called because of the cat's eyes we see on the roads at night.

The operator requesting a pick-up will merely inform the desk operator that he requires a pick-up between spot code yellow 3 and red 14. He may do this at a prearranged time, but more likely, he will call for the pick-up only when he is ready. The stretch of road between yellow 3 and red 14 may be several miles long, and this is where the cat's eyes come in. The agent simply plants his cat's eyes in the grass at the side of the road, making sure that the head is visible to oncoming traffic. The pick-up car then travels along the route between the spot codes until the driver sees the cat's eyes reflecting in the grass – at the signal, he deactivates the brake lights and stops with the rear nearside passenger open.

The agent, who by this time is lying hidden nearby, jumps to his feet, picks up the cat's eyes and gets into the car, which then drives away. The whole operation takes just seconds.

Surveillance Checklist

Preparation is the key to a successful surveillance operation. By having a checklist of objectives, manning and equipment requirements and issues to be raised at the operational briefing, many potential problems can be eliminated before any surveillance actually begins.

DEFINE OPERATION OBJECTIVES.

- Research all available information on the target.
- Obtain photographs and physical descriptions.
- Establish license numbers and make of vehicles used by target.
- List target's known associates.
- Establish whether the target is likely to be armed?
- Obtain a detailed sketch of the target's premises or an aerial photograph.
- Define points of entry and exit.
- Get hold of a detailed street map of the target's premises and the surrounding area.
- Establish codes for the target, his associates, locations and any alternate plans etc.

MANNING REQUIREMENTS

- Outline the number of surveillance operators required.
- List types of surveillance required, i.e. OP, static or mobile.
- Calculate the minimum number of vehicles required.
- Identify specific operators for individual tasks.
- Consider male/female surveillance teams and any ethnic requirement.

EQUIPMENT

- Check and test all radio equipment (both for the vehicle and for personal use). Include spare batteries.
- Issue adequate funds (including change) for telephone calls, parking, meals etc.
- Request all forms of technical equipment required, cameras, binoculars etc.
- Consider a change of clothing or disguise in vehicle.
- Develop a recovery procedure in the event of a breakdown or an accident.

- Field test all communications with base station.
- Install repeaters in areas of poor communications if required

OPERATIONAL BRIEFING

- Reiterate the problems arising from compromise to the surveillance operators.
- Emphasize the need for safe and discreet driving.
- Examine operational objectives and consider the benefits of surveillance.
- Distribute all available data, such as photographs and telephone numbers.
- Designate radio channels and repeat proper radio procedures.
- Make sure all drivers fuel their vehicles prior to any operations.
- Test and distribute any required specialist equipment.
- Go through the procedure if counter-intelligence is detected.
- Plan a familiarization run of the target's premises and the surrounding area.

There should always be a post-operational debrief which allows all those who took part in the operation to have their say. Things to be discussed should include the route taken, any deliberate stops made by the target, any photographs or video footage that have been taken. Mobile surveillance has a habit of going wrong and the debrief must deal with any points of possible compromise, as well as discussing any solutions that could be taken.

Overview of Technical Surveillance

The vast amount of technical surveillance equipment available to a surveillance unit is almost too great to catalogue. The advances in camera miniaturization and wireless communications are unprecedented.

Much of the research into military and government surveillance equipment has, after a few years, found its way on to the civilian market. There was a time when specialized equipment such as this could only be found in specialist shops. Today, it is freely available over the Internet.

Overt surveillance is everywhere. CCTV has spread through the major cities of the world, watching the traffic, the trains, the planes and you! IT technology monitors the workplace, your telephone calls are recorded and your pass is registered as you enter or leave a building. In some buildings you are actually "tagged" as you enter and are monitored as you move around. Technology can watch, monitor, record and assess your every movement. Add the specialist capabilities of a government surveillance unit to this and you would think that no one could hide – but some do. Osama Bin Laden for one, together with thousands of other terrorists.

While the armoury of electronic devices is numerous, they are and will always remain, technical devices, capable of doing only what is required of them. It may be possible to construct a camera no larger than a pinhead that can send good quality pictures around the world, but there are plenty of other things to be taken into consideration. First, the intelligence agencies must locate their target, and that is not as easy as it might sound. Secondly, they must get close enough to be able to install a technical device covertly and, finally, they must maintain it, i.e. they must change its batteries or fix it if it fails to work. When your target is hidden in a cave, deep underground and guarded by devoted followers, it presents the intelligence agencies with a difficult task.

We have all experienced the reduction in size of most electronic goods, but in the surveillance industry this has been far more prolific. Whereas in the 1950s intelligence agency technicians struggled to reduce the size of a conventional camera, today's digital versions are little more than pinheads. Nano technology is rapidly replacing miniaturization as we know it. The cameras and transmitters of tomorrow will be almost invisible to the human eye.

COUNTER-MEASURES TO TECHNICAL SURVEILLANCE

Anybody could be under surveillance, so it is important to be able to spot the telltale signs. Those who believe that they are under surveillance, or those simply suspicious of the fact, may choose to purchase, and use, specialist equipment to confirm the situation. Always remember, anything you do, write or say can be monitored by a myriad of technical devices.

To that end, there is a general list of counter measures that both the general public and spies should look out for. If you are a handler who is about to arrange a meeting with a recruited agent, or if you head a business that is about to announce a multi-million pound order – then it is realistic to suspect that some form of technical surveillance will be, or already has been, targeted against you. Here are some indicators that you are possibly under technical surveillance.

- **When you have detected mobile or static surveillance in the past, yet recently you are convinced that they have stopped watching you. They have planted and are using technical surveillance instead.**
- **You detect that all is not right in your home. Your furniture seems to have moved or your personal effects are not where you left them.**
- **Your home or office has been burgled, but nothing of significance has been stolen. This could mean a professional team has entered your premises and implanted a number of technical devices. Check for loose plasterwork or plaster crumbs. Check all electrical fittings including your phone. Check the walls and ceiling for any telltale signs or bulges. Open and check any fixed items, such a fire alarms, plug sockets, light fittings and wall clocks.**
- **The door locks are not working as smoothly as they have done for years. A good indicator that someone has been using lock-picks to gain entry. Install a dead bolt type locking system, heavy enough to stop the average locksmith. Check the external doorframe for indentations. This could mean that a hydraulic jack has been used to spread the doorframe and release the locks and bolts from their housing (see lock picking).**
- **Your phone is making odd noises; it rings and there is no one there; you can hear a tone when the phone is on the hook. All these indicate a telephone tap.**
- **The television, car radio or AM/FM radio develops strange interference. This could mean that the unit has been tampered with and that a hidden wireless**

microphone has been implanted. You might well be picking up static from a device near to the television or radio.

- **Be wary of any sales person offering you a free gift, such as a pen, a cuddly toy or a clock radio. These can all contain hidden audio-visual devices with a wireless transmitter.**
- **Take notice of any van type vehicle that has suddenly started to appear in your street. These are usually disguised as utility or trade vehicles. Check the vehicle with a walk-past. If you cannot see clearly into the whole vehicle, you must suspect that it is a technical surveillance vehicle. Use a stethoscope pressed against the windowpane to try and detect any microwave "bussing". Check for any vehicles in line of sight of the window.**
- **Never allow anyone to enter your premises without good reason. Telephone or electrical engineers, do not just "turn up". Check the identity of anyone you are not sure of. Watch them while they are working if you are suspicious.**

If you ever feel your home or premises have been violated, call your own technical people and have them do a sweep. If there is anything planted, they should be able to find it.

Audio-Visual Surveillance

One method of surveillance allows the target to be observed both audibly and visually (with photographs and videos).

Most modern devices can record both sound and pictures concurrently. The audio element provides voice patterns from which the target can be identified. The video element reveals an individual's hand and body gestures and facial expressions. Audio-visual is by far the greatest tool in the modern day surveillance arsenal.

A combination of audio-visual devices can be hidden just about anywhere, even on an unsuspecting person. Homes, offices, vehicles and even public transport are easy targets for a technical department of any good intelligence agency. Hiding a "bug" in light fittings, smoke detectors, toys, clocks, garden rocks, front doors or in the bedroom ceiling are all easily achieved.

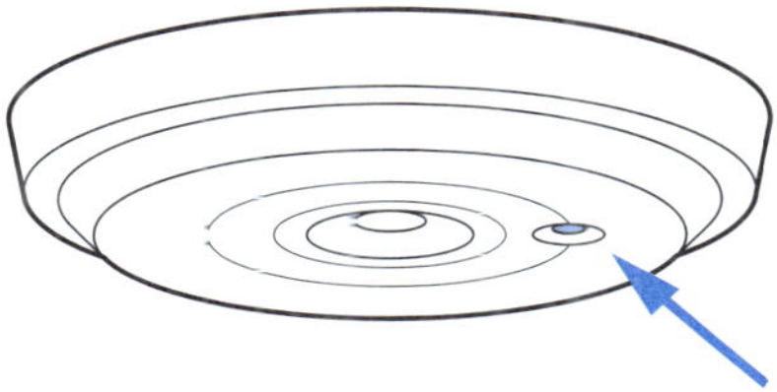

HIDING BUGS

Bugs are often hidden within inconspicuous equipment already established in the home or work place. A classic example of this practice is the bug and its battery secreted within a smoke detector.

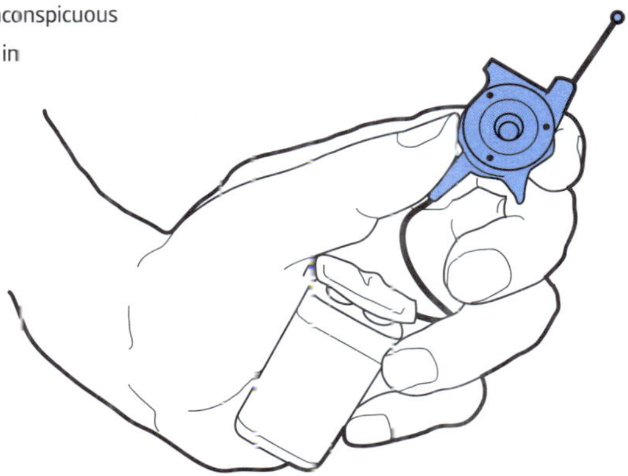

Computer Surveillance

There is hardly a home or an office these days that does not contain a computer, most of which are linked to the Internet.

For this reason, intelligence agencies regard computers as a vital element of surveillance. Computer surveillance, commonly known as "hacking" or "reading", is the ability to access a target's computer and to investigate any information that may be of a suspicious or incriminating nature.

Both PC and laptop computers can be modified in a number of ways. It is possible, for example, to fit a separate word processing system in a laptop, which, for the most part, will never be discovered. The designated user activates the system and, once finished, he simply hits a combination of keys to return the laptop to its normal state. This allows him to write and store messages outside of the laptop's normal functions, thus preventing any messages from being found if the laptop is lost or stolen.

Another system, known as SRAC (Short Range Agent Communication), allows messages written on a computer to be downloaded onto a small SRAC transmitter. This device, slightly larger than a cigarette packet, continually sends out a low power interrogation signal. When the receiving agent is close enough – about 100 m away – the SRAC transmitter makes contact automatically and "burst" transmits any waiting message.

Tracking

Tracking devices, which may vary in type, size and ability, have become both increasingly popular and extremely accurate. Even though the technology of tracking devices has improved, they should only be seen as an aid to surveillance rather than an independent stand-alone system.

SATELLITE

Satellites have been used for the purpose of intelligence gathering since the late 1950s. There are three types of imagery satellites: photographic, electro-optical and synthetic aperture radar (SAR).

Satellite images have improved dramatically over the years and definition these days is now down to just a few centimetres. The advances in satellite images for the purpose of intelligence include 3D modelling, which is done by blending images from a variety of sources. This clarity enables intelligence agencies to have a clear idea of what is happening in any part of the world at any time. This includes spotting potential spies doing a "walk through" of a city or an area before they are actually assigned to a job.

The disadvantage of satellites is their high cost and their relatively short lifespan. To help combat this, NASA is developing a new type of unmanned spy plane. These will operate some 30 km above the earth's surface and will be sustained by solar power. The aim is to try and get the new spy planes to fly in a controlled orbit at very low speeds. This combination should produce excellent imagery and should reduce the current reliance on satellites.

GPS/GSM

There have been great advances in this form of tracking. The arrival of the Global Positioning System (GPS) and the widespread use of mobile telephones provide an excellent platform for tracking.

GPS's accuracy is increasing and will continue to do so as the European "Galileo" system comes into operation in 2008. When this happens, the accuracy of a ground position will be down to mere centimetres. Likewise, the advances in mobile phone technology

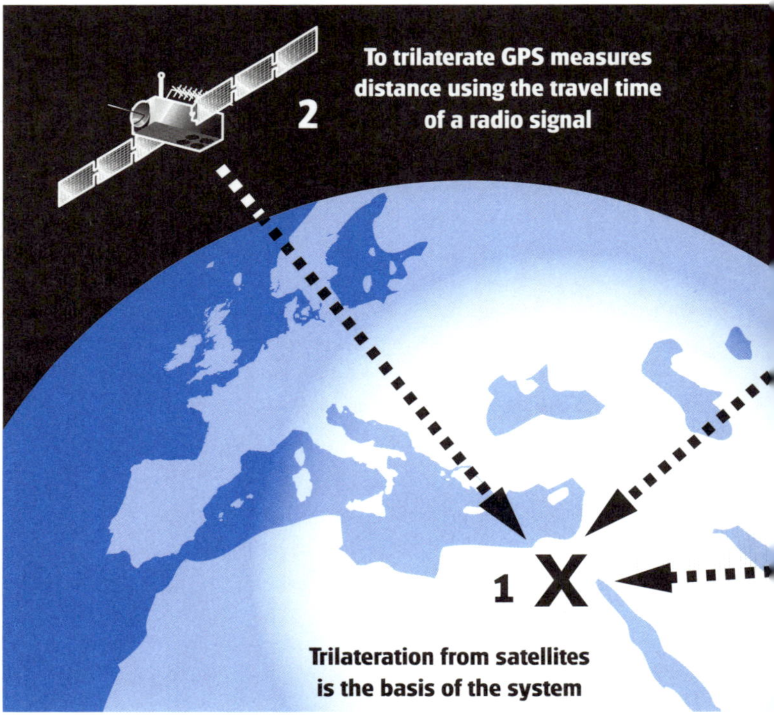

continue to race ahead and excellent coverage is now available over most of the world's populated surface.

Current GPS/Global System for Mobile Communications (GSM) tracking devices have shrunk to the size of a cigarette packet and continue to become smaller. Their signal can be transmitted over the GSM network from anywhere to anywhere. Even when a GSM signal in not available, the tracking device can store its positions until a signal can be regained. These signals transpose onto a map indicating the movement of a tracking device in real time. Tracking devices can be installed in vehicles, people or can be attached to movable objects.

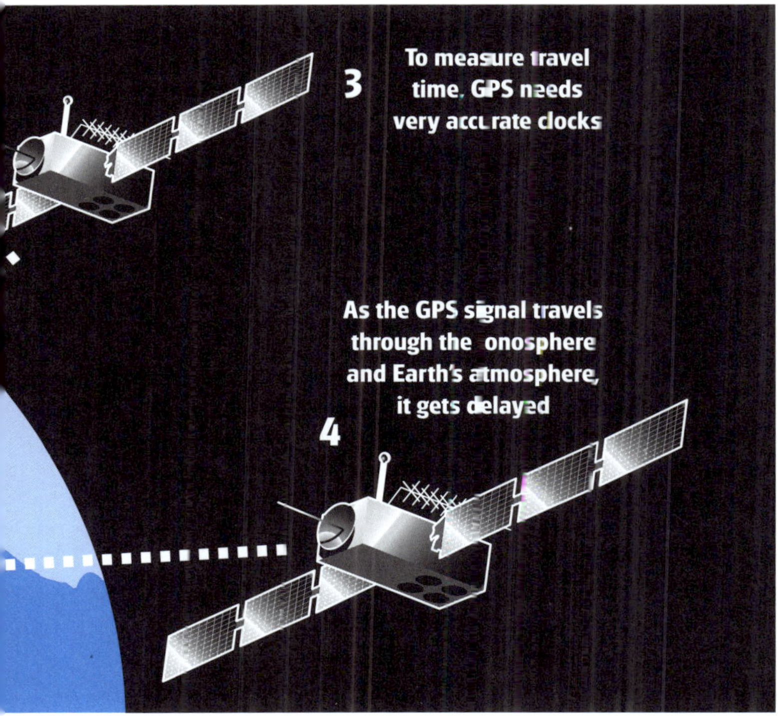

Technical Observation Equipment

There is little point in locating and constructing a good OP if you do not have the correct equipment with which to observe the target.

The surveillance operators must make a list of their technical requirements prior to entering the OP and these must enable viewing over a 24-hour period and in all weather conditions. This list may include, monoculars, binoculars, telescopes, periscopes, night vision devices, thermal imaging devices and acoustic devices. Many of these devices can produce still photography, video or audio playback. A major consideration when selecting equipment should be the range to target, the magnification requirements and current audio volume (traffic noise) between the OP and the target. The technical equipment used might include:

- **Binoculars and telescopes**
- **Conventional and digital cameras**
- **Analog and digital video cameras**
- **Night vision equipment**
- **Pinhole and microcircuit cameras**
- **Wireless and remote image transmission technology**

BINOCULARS AND TELESCOPES

Binoculars and telescopes are still one of the best surveillance aids available today. It is always a good idea to have a small pair of binoculars to hand, either on your person or in the surveillance vehicle. Binoculars are quick to acquire a moving target; on the other hand, telescopes, which are often mounted, are much slower.

The Eyeball vs. Technology

Never forget that the equipment is only an aid when it comes to surveillance; the "mark one" eyeball is still the best observation device.

Modern telescopes are extremely powerful and capable of immense magnification. They are generally used in the OP, whether in a rural or an urban location. The secret to selecting the correct telescope is to assess the range to the target and to define the definition required. While it is often too easy to select a very powerful telescope, this can pose several problems; the first is one of stabilization. If your telescope is too powerful, the target image will appear "shaky" and you will not be able to read target detail correctly.

CONVENTIONAL AND DIGITAL CAMERAS

Until the 1950s, cameras were the epitome of surveillance. The only other reasonable source of technical information came from a telephone tap. There is much truth in the saying "a picture is worth a thousand words", as a camera can capture a single moment in time. In surveillance terms, that may be the moment when the target's identity is established or when you discover his association with another. Whatever the case, it provides a lasting image for others to examine.

The first "spy" camera was little more than a normal camera reduced in size; it required film, which in turn required processing. While this may be an over-simplification, there have been some wonderful and ingenious adaptations over the years. Surveillance or "spy" cameras were to be found hidden in books or vehicles, they were sometimes used in Ops, with a telephoto lens attached. These "conventional" cameras produced outstanding quality in their definition clarity. They could also be adapted for use in total darkness by using infrared. Then along came the digital age.

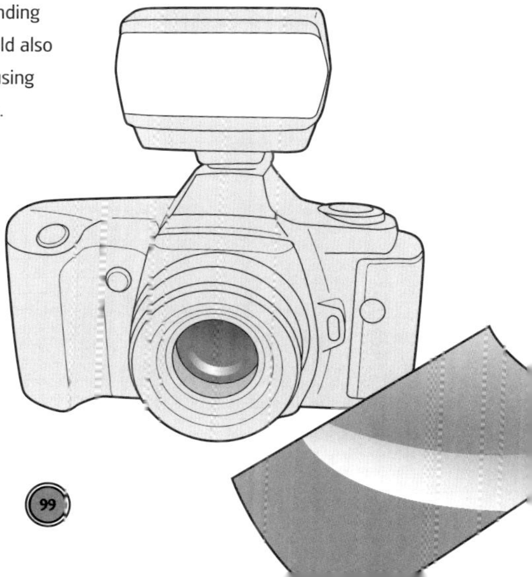

INFRARED (IR)

It is possible to convert a normal SLR camera into an infrared camera. The process is fairly easy and, in the absence of any other night vision camera, is worth knowing. It requires the purchase of two items – a gelatine filter and a high-speed infrared film.

Use the face of the camera flash to mark out a rough template of the flash lens. Remove a sheet of the Kodak gelatine filter, holding it by the edge, and place it on the template paper. Cut around the template leaving a generous overlap. Fix masking tape to the edge of the gelatine template and secure it over the lens flash.

Make sure that you are in total darkness and insert a roll of Kodak HIE 36 high-speed infrared film into the camera. You are now ready to take pictures in complete darkness.

Don't forget to pre-focus your camera, as you will not be able to see in the darkness. For example, if your intention is to take pictures of documents or maps, pre-focus in daylight and make a measuring stick. It is then a simple matter of placing your stick on the centre of the document and your camera on the other end, hold the camera still, remove the stick and take your pictures.

Developing IR Photographs

Although it has diminished with the advancement of digital cameras, developing photographs is still a required tradecraft skill. While this should be done under ideal conditions, the spy often has to improvise. The following is a basic method for developing infrared film. You will need to purchase some basic photographic chemical and equipment. Many photographic shops sell basic kits that contain just about everything you need, including a set of instructions. There are two stages in producing a photograph from a roll of film: firstly, developing the film and, secondly, developing the picture from the film.

DEVELOPING THE FILM

In doing this you will require a developing tank. This is a small, black plastic tank with a reel inside. Unscrew the top and remove the reel. Lay the parts out so that you can identify them in the dark. You will note that the top and bottom of the reel move in different directions for about 5 cm. There is also an inner edge, into which the film is threaded.

Prepare your developer. This is done by adding warm water – around 28°C – to the quantity specified on the label. You will need enough water to cover the film when it is in the tank. Also prepare your stop solution and your fixing agent, again as described on the instruction label.

The following process must take place in total darkness. Remove the film from the camera and pull some 30 cm of it free. Feed this end into the reel, there is a start point that you can feel with your fingers. Once the film is partly in, the two parts of the reel will feed in the rest of the film.

Place the reel into the tank, screw on the top and then pour in the developer. A paddle stick is provided with the tank that fits through a hole in the top and clips into the reel. Use this for agitating the film while in the tank. Develop the film for six minutes and 45 seconds before emptying out the developer. Insert the stop solution and agitate for one-and-a-half minutes before emptying out the solution. Pour in the fixing agent and agitate for five minutes. Then pour the fixing agent out.

Your film will now be developed. Unscrew the top and place the open tank under a running tap for several minutes in order to remove any chemicals. Once this has been done, take out the reel and slowly remove the developed film. Use clothes pegs to weight the roll open and hang it in a clean warm place to dry. The careful use of a hairdryer will speed up the process.

While the film is drying, prepare three flat trays, filling them with 5 cm of developer, stop and fixer. As the negatives are small, you will need an enlarger in order to print out a picture that can be viewed easily.

Once your film is dry, cut it into manageable strips of four to six exposures. Place a strip in the enlarger and manoeuvre it until the desired exposure is visible on the enlarger board. Adjust both the height and the focus to the desired size then switch off the enlarger and place a sheet of contact paper on the board. Expose for five seconds by switching on the enlarger lamp. Remove, the contact paper and place in the developer dish. Agitate by hand until the picture is visible and sharp. Remove from the developer and place it for one minute in the stop solution. Finally, place the picture in the fixing agent for five minutes before removing it, washing it in clean water and hanging it up to dry. You can experiment with both exposure and developer timings in order to achieve the best results.

DIGITAL

Digital cameras today are, in terms of quality, capable of taking near-perfect photographs, the results of which can be viewed instantly. Most are capable of running rapid sequences or full video, albeit at a lower resolution. While these features are a major asset to any surveillance operator, their true capabilities come from the fact that they are digital. This means that, when it comes to taking or transmitting images, a digital camera can be controlled electronically. A digital camera can be disguised as a rock and placed in your front garden. It can take pictures day or night on command or by sensor activation. These pictures can then be downloaded by radio frequency, over the Internet or via the GSM network. Most digital cameras used for surveillance are available commercially. If there is an adaptation, it is simply in their usage, that is to say they are disguised in one form or another.

NIGHT VISION SYSTEMS

Night vision systems range from miniature "pocketscopes" to large, tripod-mounted models. The present range of third generation image intensifiers, which can operate with virtually no available light, can be adapted to suit various phases of surveillance; individual weapon sights (IWS), night observation devices (NODs) and night vision goggles (NVGs). All should be available during the various stages of surveillance depending on the requirements for the moment; be it a target recce NVG, a NOD observation or IWS if a night assault phase is required.

Thermal imagers can also be supplied for surveillance and target acquisition during night and day. A number of different models, varying in size from hand-held types to tripod-mounted devices coaxially mounted with laser rangefinders, are available. When the target is obscured by weather, smoke, dust or any other form of masking, thermal imagers have the distinct advantage over image intensifiers, as they work on heat detection. Depending on the type and model, night vision devices can work over distances up to several thousand metres.

LISTENING DEVICES

As is the case with audio-visual devices, there is an unbelievable amount of listening devices available for surveillance. They range from straightforward bugging devices hidden in a building or in a vehicle to microwave or laser beams that are aimed at a window. No matter which device is used, the most important aspect with any system is to anticipate where the best reception can be achieved and balance this with placing the correct device in the best possible position.

The best position for a listening device depends on the target's social habits. That is to say, does he spend a lot of time in the home, in the office or driving his car? While he may spend several hours a day in his car, is he alone? Drivers don't generally talk to themselves while driving. The original target recce should provide an insight as to the best place to fit a listening device. For example, if the family gathers in the kitchen, this would be an obvious location. Alternatively, if the target spends eight hours a day sitting at an office desk, this may also prove a good opportunity to use a listening device. In the final event, a full range of listening devices may be deployed in order to monitor most of the target's conversation.

How Night Vision Works

There are two forms of night vision, image intensifier (light amplification) and thermal imaging (infrared). Image intensifiers take small amounts of light, (starlight and moonlight) and convert the light photons into electrons. These electrons are then multiplied inside the image intensifier tube before being converted back into photons. This provides the viewer with a clear night vision image that would be impossible for the human eye. The process of most image intensifiers causes the viewed image to appear green, a distinctive characteristic of night vision.

The first operational night vision appeared in the mid-1960s and was used extensively in the Vietnam War. These could be hand-held or used on a weapon. They have progressed by generation, the latest being Generation 3. The photocathode in Gen 3 enables vastly increased viewing distance under near total darkness. Because an image intensifier emits no beam, it is known as "passive" night vision.

Thermal imaging has been around since the 1940s, but it was overtaken by the introduction of image intensifiers – until the shortcomings of the latter became obvious. In certain operations, a thermal imager is very much superior to an image intensifier, as it can locate human or structural images that would be obscured to image intensifiers by smoke, cloud, mist or snow to name just a few. Because they need to emit a beam of infrared light, they are known as "proactive" night vision.

4 METHODS OF ENTRY

Methods of entry (MoE) cover a wide variety of spycraft skills, which fall into two categories – covert (gaining access) and overt (making access). If a spy wishes to plant a bug in the target's house, he will most probably wish to enter the premises and leave covertly. In contrast, a raid on a suspected terrorist bomb-making factory would almost certainly be initiated by the use of force that will inevitably result in a loud noise at the point of entry.

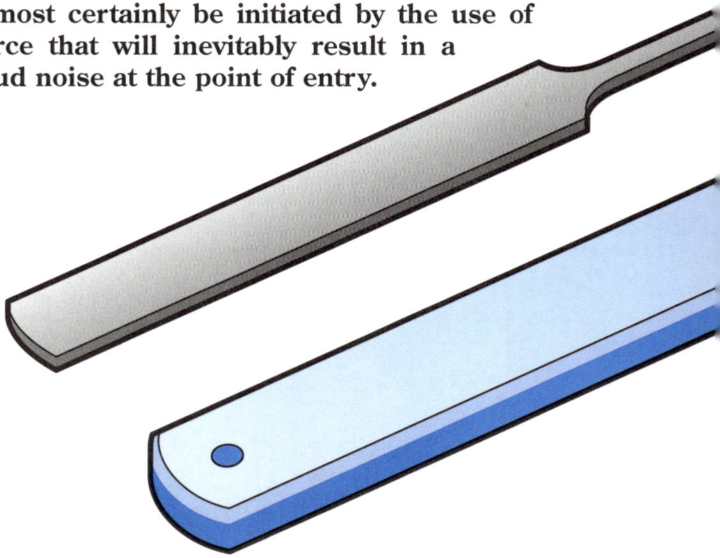

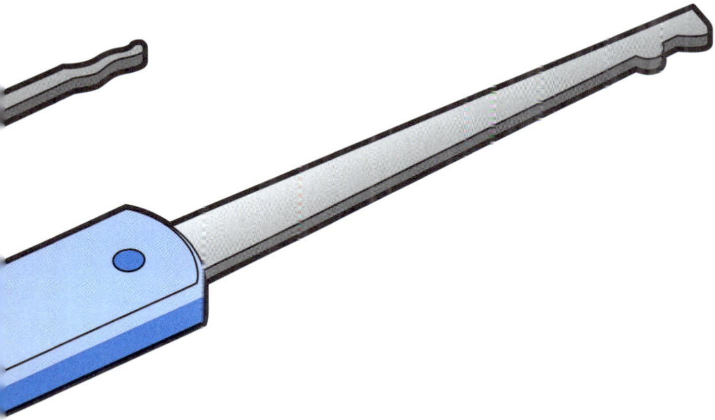

Disclaimer

All of the information and techniques explained in this section are in the public domain. They outline the skills of secret agents and Special Forces operating in foreign countries. The section on lock picking is merely an outline and the skills required to perfect the art take years to master.

In its basic form, infiltration is simply gaining access to a structure, whether it is a building, an aircraft, a ship or a vehicle. To gain access, a spy may have to climb up, abseil down or carry out direct penetration, i.e. he may need to go through a wall. Much of the equipment required for MoE is termed "low tech", and, for the most part, has been developed through necessity or constant civilian usage. Counter-terrorist techniques have turned the humble builder's ladder into a rapid means of access, while much of the cutting equipment used has been developed from items similar to those used on a day-to-day basis by the rescue services.

Other more specialist MoE skills use a mixture of military and civilian techniques; these include lock picking and the use of explosives. Covert entry can be made by picking the locks, or by silently cutting through steel bars or doors. Overt entry, on the other hand, is normally carried out using the fastest methods – through the use of explosives or wall-breaching cannons.

When access to a house or building is required, the agents will normally carry out a target recce (*see* Surveillance section). This entails a simple observation of the premises to establish the correct address, the main points of entry and to ascertain the time when the property is occupied. Once this basic information has been collated a method of entry will then be formulated. Depending on the security devices protecting the house, a plan will be made to either break in – and make it look as though a burglary has taken place – or to effect a covert entry.

Surprising as it may seem, it is often better to carry out a target during daylight hours, especially if you intend it to look like a robbery. At ten in the morning, the man of the house is likely to be at work, the children are probably at school and the wife could well be out shopping. In contrast, a house is almost always occupied from six in the evening and throughout the night.

Alarms

All but a few alarms are controlled by a four-digit code that is punched into a box conveniently situated somewhere close to the main point of entry. This allows the property owner a short period of time to enter the house and to deactivate the alarm.

Alarm systems are designed to activate under certain conditions; for the most part when one of the internal sensors has detected somebody's presence or when a door or window contact has been broken. This activates the alarm and the box on the outside of the building is set off. In some cases the alarm may phone the local police (they will only accept VIPs), or even the house owner's mobile phone.

There are several ways of bypassing an alarm system. For example, you could get a ladder and insert expanding foam (available from any DIY store) into the outside alarm box, remembering to break the light if one is attached. A better method is to identify the alarm system manufacturer and then obtain the engineer's shutdown code.

While both of these methods are effective, the modern agent should have a small plate-like device at his disposal (the name of which is classified) that he simply places over the keys on the control box and which will display the correct code instantly. The device measures the pressure of the push buttons, as each is minutely different. The pad is sensitive enough to measure the difference (and will also determine the order) in which the four code keys are pressed. The device works on around 70 per cent of known keypads.

The best way of carrying out daylight entry is by walking up to the front door and knocking loudly (do not rely on the doorbell as it may be broken), in order to establish whether anyone is at home. If someone answers the door, then simply switch to a back-up plan – say that you are collecting for charity, for example. If no one is at home, you may wish to enter the premises directly, by forcing the door with a wrecking bar or, if the property is hidden from view, use a hydraulic spreader. Another alternative is to go to the rear of the house and to try there. Try not to break glass; it has a nasty habit of making a distinctive sound that could arouse the suspicion of any neighbours.

Once entry has been affected, you should consider the amount of time that it will take to plant bugs and to search the place. If you have forced your way into the property, then make it look like a burglary; if you have entered covertly, make sure that you don't disturb anything. If the house is not under observation from a static OP, you would be well advised to have a sentry posted outside to provide a warning if anyone should return to the property.

MOE CONSIDERATIONS

- Always check around the property and take all possible points of entry into consideration. Almost two-thirds of all burglaries take place through unlocked windows and doors.
- Check under the mat, flowerpot, the nearest garden stone or gnome and peer through the letterbox for a length of string – you would be surprised where people hide keys.
- Street lights often illuminate the front or rear of a property, use an air rifle to take them out a couple of nights before you intend to enter. Do not just do one, knock out several in the same street to avoid suspicion.
- The doors are one of the most common means of entry. They are also the most protected, however. Remember that the front door normally controls any alarm system, so you must either deactivate the alarm externally or, enter through this door and then deactivate the alarm. Entering at any other point will instantly trigger the alarm.

- Given their accessibility, windows are the most vulnerable point of entry. However, one should always bear in mind the fact that glass makes a sharp, distinctive noise when it is broken.
- Sliding glass doors provide an easy point of entry as their locks are notoriously poor; some 50 percent of them refuse to lock after a couple of years' usage. In addition, they can easily be lifted off their tracks and removed totally.
- Make a note of any fences that surround the property. If they are high, locate the entry and exit points in the event that you need to make a quick getaway.
- Don't bother with roof hatches unless the property is a large industrial unit or similar type of building.
- Cellar or basement apartments are an ideal point of entry, and while many are self-contained, there is generally a way up into the main house. Basements will give you the time you need to pick locks or to force an entry undetected.
- Garages and tool sheds may not be your main target of attack, but they are generally easy to enter. They will provide you with a great deal of equipment – from ladders to cordless drills – that can be used to affect entry in an emergency.

Spiderman Suckers

Spiderman suckers allow the user to climb up vertical walls with a great degree of safety. The four vacuum pads will adhere to any surface, be it concrete, sandstone, plaster, wood, glass or metal. Each pad is computer controlled, which means that the vacuum effect of each pad can be constantly measured and adjusted. A visual and acoustic warning signal informs the user about the load carrying capacity of each pad and a fail-safe method ensures that only one pad can be removed at any time.

The unit is operated using compressed air supplied by an air cylinder that is worn on the operator's back. The air cylinder allows approximately two hours of climbing time. The total unit weight is about 25 kg, and offers a carrying capacity of around one metric tonne. Training to use the device takes about one hour and, with practice, the operator can learn to climb overhangs.

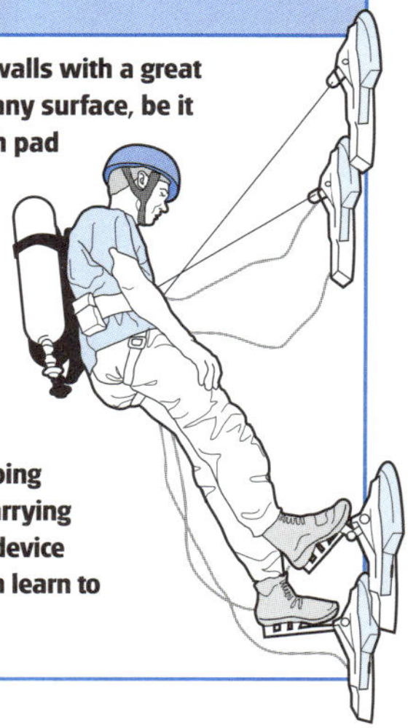

Rapid Entry Equipment

Once a person has climbed or abseiled into position, they will require a means of gaining entry.

Once a person has climbed or abseiled into position, they will require a means of gaining entry. Rapid entry equipment ranges from silent hydraulic cutters and spreaders to sledge hammers, crowbars and axes. These tools are commonly known in UK intelligence circles to as a "Barclaycard", meaning an entry tool that works particularly well for gaining quick access into a building. Most hydraulic tools use lightweight pumps that can be easily carried by one man. The following are a cross section of the equipment available:

- A **Manual Door Ram** is a hand-held ram designed to force inward-opening doors. The ram is swung against the lock area and imparts a weight load of approximately three tons. It is effective against all but reinforced steel doors and weighs 16 kg.
- A **Door ripper** is a lightweight tool designed to force outward-opening doors. The blade of the tool is driven between the door and the frame in the lock area. A ratchet mechanism helps overcome resistance by allowing the blade to be worked behind the door thus providing increased force.
- A **Hydraulic Door Ram** is designed to force reinforced inward-opening doors. It is supplied with three sets of claws to suit all standard widths of door from 760 mm to 920 mm. The main ram is positioned over the lock area while the secondary ram forces the jaws into the frame. A valve then activates the main ram to force the door open exerting a maximum force of five tons. An 11-ton version is also available.
- The **Hooligan bar** is an American-designed rapid entry tool. Essentially, it is a one metre metal bar with various attachments. Two or three blows with the bar will take out most of the window; the hooks are then used to pull out the debris or can be used as leverage on sash-type windows.
- **Spreaders** are used to either lift a door off its hinges or to lift or move a heavy object.
- **Jaws** and **disk cutters** are used to cut or penetrate any form of metal. Some hydraulic models can cut metal bars that are up to 35 mm thick.

Thermal Lance

The thermal lance is designed for cutting mild steel, including objects that are underwater.

The basic system consists of a 12-foot flexible thermal lance made from Kerie cable, a single three-litre oxygen cylinder fitted with pressure gauges, a pressure regulator, a battery-powered igniter and a three-way valve which switches the system's working pressure on or off. Once ignited, the Kerie cable burns at approximately two feet a minute during cutting, and has a maximum cutting time of six minutes. A backpack portable system that weighing 10.5 kg is favoured for cutting during a covert entry.

Lock Picking

All agents need to learn the basics of lock picking as part of their tradecraft.

The principle of picking locks is fairly basic, as are lock-picking tools, the majority of which can be easily made or improvised. The problem with picking locks lies in the skill. It can take many years to perfect the fundamentals of lock picking and it is a skill that requires constant practice in order to adapt the "feel". A very brief guide to the lock picking process is outlined below.

LOCK PICKING EQUIPMENT

There is a wide range of lock picking equipment on the market. These include the traditional lock picking sets to the more advanced lock-pick guns. The basic lock-pick set consists of a range of tools including several different lock-pick shapes and a variety of tension bars. Most sets will also include tools for the removal of broken keys.

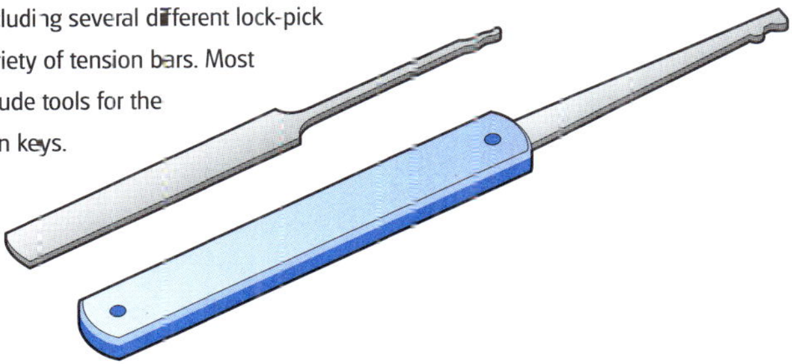

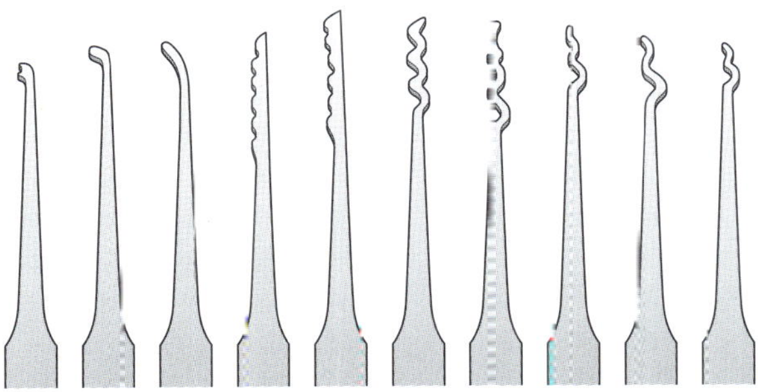

There are many different types of lock picking guns available to the agent, but these are generally bulky by comparison to the lock-pick set. Lock-pick guns are available in either manual or electric operation, and all have interchangeable picks. Whilst the Cobra Electronic lock pick is often acclaimed as the ultimate device, the Lockaid gun is far more efficient and reliable.

PIN TUMBLER LOCK

Most of the locks manufactured over the past 20 years are of the pin tumbler type. In its basic form, it is a very simple locking device. A series of small pins fit into the inner barrel of a cylinder. The pins are split in the middle, normally at different lengths and are forced into recesses within the inner barrel by a small spring. If a correct key is inserted, the different sized pins are brought into line where their split meets in the outer casing of the inner barrel. This allows the inner barrel to turn freely within the casing and the lock is then released.

Any method of aligning the pins in this manner and turning the inner barrel will open the lock. This can be achieved by two methods – racking or picking the pins. To achieve this, two basic tools are required – a lock pick or a rake and a tension bar. The pick, or rake, is a flat strip of hardened metal that has had its end shaped to fit into the lock and which advances the pins on their small springs to the required depth. The tension bar is a flat strip of metal inserted into the mouth of the barrel to employ a minute amount of tension onto it. This process helps seat the pins and turn the barrel.

Note: While most locks turn clockwise, some cylinders may well turn the opposite way. If the tumbler's pins will not break, or if they stay broken, it means that you are applying tension in the wrong direction. If you can hear several clicks once the tension has been released, it means that you are turning the tumbler in the right direction.

RAKING AND PICKING

There are many different types and designs of lock picking tools and they can all be used for different functions. I would suggest that two are sufficient. Raking is the quickest method of opening a lock. It is fast and straightforward providing that the pin sizes do not change suddenly. However, before you start, make sure that the lock is clean and free from any grit or dirt. Blowing hard into the lock before attempting to open it is a good idea. Raking involves inserting the pick to the rear of the pins and swiftly snapping the pick outwards, running the tip over the pins in the process.

Prior to doing this, a tension bar is inserted into the bottom of the keyway and a slight pressure is applied on the lock's inner barrel. The tension is applied in the unlock direction. The amount of tension exerted should just be enough to turn the barrel once the pins are seated, but not so strong as to bind the pins against the barrel. It is this single "feel" that is the basis of all good lock picking. If the tension is too heavy, the top pins will bind and the searline will not allow the breaking point to meet. If it is too weak, the pins will simply fall back into the locked position.

When raking, you will have to repeat the operation several times. If the barrel does not turn by the fourth time, hold the tension in place with the tool. Place your ear to the lock and slowly release the tension, if you hear the pitting sound as the pins fall back to rest, then you have applied too much pressure. If you hear nothing, then you need to apply more pressure on the tension bar.

The ease at which a lock can be opened will depend on three things: firstly the length and position of the pins, secondly the type of tools you use, and thirdly, the make of the lock. Cheap locks will be easier to open than expensive ones. Cheaper locks are generally poorly constructed, allowing for a much greater clearance between the barrel and the body, thus making it far easier to assemble during manufacture. Cheap locks can also have poor barrel alignment and oversized pin holes – both of which make it a very easy lock to pick.

Lock picking is very similar to raking, but it requires a lot more skill, as the pins need to be seated individually. Starting at the back of the lock, feel for the rear most pin and gently push it up, the barrel should move a fraction. Working towards the end of the lock, seat each pin in turn until the barrel is released. A combination of one swift rake followed by picking is sometimes the easy answer to cracking the lock.

One of the reasons some pins bind or stick is that the top is often mushroom-shaped, causing the top to topple and bind on the searline. Careful picking will overcome this. One particular make of lock, called Medeco, splits the pins on an angle; making it a very difficult lock to pick.

In an emergency, it is possible to bypass the pins by drilling a line through the lock. You must direct the drill towards the top centre of the lock where the tumbler meets the body. It is best to use a centre punch to provide the drill with a good start guide. Drill straight through for at least three centimetres. You will need to push a screwdriver into the keyhole in order to turn the lock.

You can develop the feel for lock picking by doing a daily exercise. Wash your hands and then rub in some hand cream. Massage both your hands and your fingers for about five minutes and then let them relax. Find a smooth surface, such as a sheet of glass, an old picture frame is perfect, and place a few grains of sugar on the surface of it. Close your eyes and gently use your fingers to locate the grains of sugar. When you have done so play with each one of them very gently. See if you can differentiate the size and shape of each grain. This exercise not only helps your feel, but it also helps your mind to visualize what you are feeling. Visualization is the key to understanding the techniques of lock picking.

Note: It is also worth sharpening one end of your pick to a needlepoint. If this point is forced all the way to the rear of a padlock – until it hits the rear plate – the sharpened pick will grip the metal. Try forcing the plate either up or down as this will sometimes release the lock without the need for raking or picking.

CLANDESTINE LOCK PICKING TIPS

- Define the lock type and its make during the target recce phase. Purchase a similar lock and practise beforehand. If you have both the time and the tools, carefully cut the lock open and examine its inner mechanics in detail.
- Some locks take time to pick, so remember to take short breaks to rest your fingers. If you do not do so will impede your ability to feel the pins.
- Avoid scratching the outer face of the lock.
- Always return the lock to its natural state once you have finished. Leaving the pins in a "floating" position will inhibit the key being placed in the lock.
- Yale, Dexter and Schlage keyways are cut at an angle. Make sure you tilt your pick to compensate and follow that angle.
- Well-made locks are extremely hard to pick; they are very tight and require a little more tension. A "springy" pin is not aligned.
- If the lock is open but the door is not you have most probably encountered internal dead
- bolts. Your best option is to use hydraulic spreaders in the door jam. Bear in mind, however, that this is likely to leave large, telltale marks.
  Most locks can be opened, but not all of them are easy. Some people have a natural ability
- for lock picking, while others struggle.

MAKE YOUR OWN LOCK PICKING SET

You will need to purchase several strips of high-tensile metal measuring 12 cm x 5 mm. These can be purchased from a model shop. Alternatively, buy a set of heavy-duty feeler gauges that are used by the motor industry. Look on the Internet for a template for lock picks and print out a sharp copy on sticky-backed paper. Next, carefully cut out the shapes and peel off the backing. Place each individual template onto a separate strip of metal or on one of the leaves of the feeler gauge. It is now a simple matter of grinding down the metal until the desired shape has been achieved. This is best done by placing the metal in a vice and grinding it with a coarse grinder to get a rough outline, before using a fine grinder to finish off. Finally, remove the paper template to reveal your pick.

It is best to place the tension bar in a vice and heat it with a blowtorch. Once the metal is hot, use a pair of pliers to twist the top 15 mm of the bar to a 90 degree turn. Then bend this over at 90 degrees to the upright section. To start with you only need to make three basic tools, as these will open 50 percent of all locks.

EMERGENCY PICKS

You can use any type of thin metal for makeshift picks and tension bars in an emergency. The best two items to use are heavy-duty paper clips or safety pins. These can easily be straightened or bent in order to make all the tools you may need to open a lock. However, they are limited to such items as lockers, draws and filing cabinets, as heavy-duty locks will require a more substantial set of tools to pick.

There are several new types of lock picks available. One is called the fibre pick. This looks and acts very much like a toothbrush, but is used to brush the lock pins instead of your teeth. Fibre locks come in a variety of different fibre sizes and strengths and it is just a matter of selecting the right fibre pick to suit your purposes.

OPENING A VEHICLE DOOR

One simple way to open a vehicle door is to use a strip of plastic banding tape – the type used to secure new box items such as televisions or washing machines. You will need about half a metre in length, and this should then be folded in half, making sure to crease the folded end.

Use a flat piece of metal – a spoon handle is perfect – to prise the vehicle door open at the top corner of the door that is furthest away from the wing mirror. This should provide you with enough space to slip in the creased end of your plastic tape. Push it about 10–12 centimetres, and, using a sawing action, pull the tape down until it is resting close to the internal door release catch. It often helps to keep the spoon in the door, as this makes it easy for the tape to slide into position. Once in position, push one end of the tape inwards while holding the other end firm; this causes the tape to form a bow near the crease. Work the tape back and forth until the bow is over the release catch. Pull the two ends of the tape tight and lift at the same time. This should unlock the door.

5 INFILTRATION

Planning any clandestine operation requires expertise, experience and a complete understanding of the operational task. For the agent or the special forces unit this is generally expressed as the "mission". Before any mission can start, however, there needs to be planning phase; this will involve acquiring knowledge of the terrain, the prevailing weather conditions and, finally, the implementation of infiltration and exfiltration methods.

Factors Influencing Infiltration

- The type of mission to be undertaken is the first thing that is taken into consideration when it comes to selecting the means of infiltration.
- The target dispositions may restrict certain means of infiltration.
- Unfavourable weather.
- The topography of the land needs be considered.
- Hydrographical factors, such as tide-data, the depth of offshore water and the location of reefs and sandbars can all influence the selection of water as a means of infiltration.
- The number of personnel being infiltrated may be a limiting factor, as will the distance if part of the way is to be made on foot.
- The equipment required in order to carry out the operation successfully may also determine the infiltration method selected.

STEALTH TECHNOLOGY

Stealth is the simple act of trying to hide or evade detection. It is not so much a technology as a concept that incorporates a broad series of technologies and design features. Stealth technology is a prime goal for most military organizations, including the intelligence agencies. Stealth enables you to sneak up on the target undetected. Militarily, this catches the target unawares, giving you the advantage of surprise while seriously impeding both the target's resistance and defences. In the past, this would have been achieved through camouflage and concealment, but modern stealth technologies mean that in many instances the target cannot respond at all, because they simply cannot see you.

Stealth clothing has been a desirable asset on the battlefield for a long time, especially for special forces infiltrating behind enemy lines. This has been achieved to some degree. One British firm in Cardiff discovered that shredded foil, similar to that used for insulation, could be used to blank out any thermal or infrared signature. This provided perfect night-time camouflage for both soldiers and tanks. However, the insulation material caused the body to overheat and the suits had to be fitted with a cooling system. Despite these drawbacks, the race is on to produce a real day-night stealth system that is suitable for both men and machines.

Overcoming Sensors

Any sensing system, whether it is an electric fence or a seismic device, can be overcome by creating an error of reasoning. The easiest way to approach this is to have a long piece of rope with a large metal object tied to the end. This is thrown at the electric fence or onto the area where known seismic probes are buried. The result will be an investigation by the border patrol. Some borders are monitored by camera, so make sure that you operate from a concealed position. Once the patrol has come and gone, repeat the process. If this is done during a storm, or during a period of high wind activity, the border guards will eventually turn off that sector or ignore the alarms, putting it down to faulty equipment.

6 CLANDESTINE OPERATIONS

A clandestine operation is any form of operation undertaken by one government against another foreign power. These operations are normally conducted in enemy-held, enemy-controlled or politically sensitive territory. Operations that are both covert and that entail a final assault mode are known as "black ops".

These are normally carried out by military personnel seconded to an intelligence agency, and are approved with the purpose of stabilizing or destabilizing the current ruling power, or to prepare the ground for an invasion.

The means by which this is done may include: supporting an opposition group, assassination, sabotage, deception or psychological warfare.

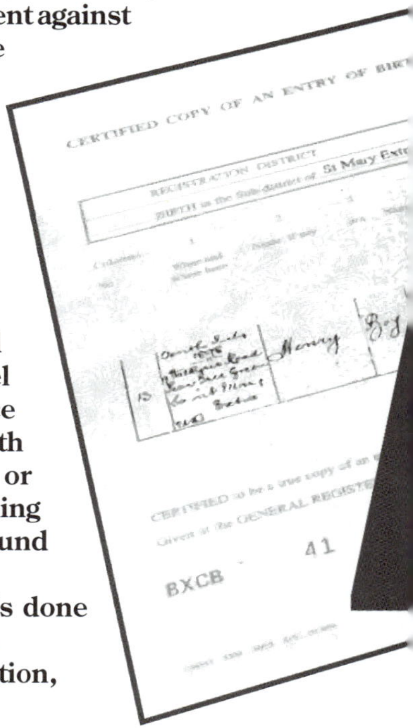
CERTIFIED COPY OF AN ENTRY OF
REGISTRATION DISTRICT
Henry
41
BXCB

EUROPEAN UNION
NITED KINGDOM OF
GREAT BRITAIN
NORTHERN IRELAND
SSPORT
South Stoneham
County of Southampton
20
TWENTY
100
IN GOD WE TRUST
TWENTY DOLLARS

Forgery

Spies and agents engaged in subversive operations are often obliged to use false documents. These include passports, identity cards and birth certificates.

Counterfeit money is also produced in large quantities and is used by many agents, often as a means of subversion. Most intelligence agencies refer to this type of forgery as "repro" with the person who makes the forgeries known as an "artist". Most agencies have their own department of "artists" who acquire documents that can be tailored to fit the agent for any special operation. Of these, by far the most important document is the passport.

Passports

It is fairly easy for an agency to obtain blank passports in their own country; it is even possible to build a complete identity for the agent. However this is not so easy to achieve when the agent is forced to operate under the guise of a foreign passport. Outside of the intelligence agency's specialized staff, it is not easy to make a forged foreign passport; the best method is to obtain a legitimate one.

A New Passport

The secret to making a new identity is to steal one from someone who is dead. The more recent the death, the better your chances are of accomplishing this. You will need to scour the obituaries and look for someone of the same race, age and gender as yourself. It is best to look in a large city, where the death rate is more numerous than in a country village. Once you have located a match, you will need to gather information about the deceased, and, if possible, obtain a photograph. The deceased's address can normally be gleaned from the newspaper, and if the death is very recent there is nothing to stop you from going along to the house and pretending to be an old friend. Once there, simply ask for a recent photograph as a keepsake. If you discover that the deceased lived alone, you might try a little burglary; if you are lucky you might even turn up the passport or birth certificate (relatives normally dig these out when someone has died). Be careful not to steal anything else. Another scam is to pretend to be a representative of the local coroner's office – make sure that you have a fake ID – and make an appointment to visit the family. If you do this, make sure that your telephone call is made just after the coroner's office closing time, so that no back check on you. Mention that you will need to see any relevant documents the family can find, such as the social security number, passport or birth certificate etc. As most people rarely deal with the coroner's office, they will think that this is a normal procedure.

If neither a burglary nor a scam failed to produce a birth certificate or a passport, then you will have to think about making and obtaining false documents. This is not as big a problem as it might seem. Once you have obtained a photograph of the deceased and have established their details it is a fairly simple matter. However, it is a task that comes with risks. You will need to obtain a legitimate copy of the deceased's birth certificate and then apply for a new passport, this time using your own photographs.

In many cases, the deceased may not look anything like you, but this is not a real problem. The secret here is to use a computer-morphing programme. Scan a facial picture of both yourself and the deceased, then, using the morphing programme, merge them halfway. The final result should look something like you. Print out four good passport photographs using photographic quality paper from any computer shop. Include these with your new passport application.

If you managed to get a copy of the deceased's passport, you can change the identity by requesting a second one from the passport office. Many countries will issue a second passport for business purposes, but you will need to prove this. One way is to update your present passport with lots of fake travel visas. You can easily copy foreign visa stamps from one passport to another. First, get a flat tray and fill it with half an inch of gelatine; let this set. Next, place a page of the passport you wish to copy onto the gelatine; do not press too hard, as this will leave an impression. Simply place a clean page from your new passport over the same area and you will pick up a copy. Simply repeat the process using a clear area of gelatine for each visa.

You will end up assuming the identity of the deceased. Providing you use your new identity in a foreign country, the chances of discovery are minimal. You will be able to open bank accounts, buy a home and do pretty much anything you like.

There are many other ways of obtaining a false passport. Stealing one while abroad is probably the easiest way, although this will be reported and cancelled. Another way is to purchase a flight ticket under a false name, have some form of ID – but not a passport– this is best done through a travel agent. You then claim to have had your passport and wallet stolen. Go to the local embassy with four photographs of yourself and ask for a new one, stating that you are leaving the country the next day; explain your flight ticket is all the proof you have. With a little luck, you will get your passport without too much hassle.

ID Cards

Identity cards, such as a driving license, do not pose a serious problem as they are much easier to forge. There are many Internet sites offering a whole range of identity cards. Few of these are any good, however. You would be better off making your own, and all your require is a modern computer set-up and a scanner. Here is how you can make a fake copy of just about any paper object.

Scan the document using a high resolution – at least 600 dpi (dots per inch) – and always in colour. This will create a large file, so you will need a good computer and graphics package to handle it. Once you have your copy, manipulate it to suit your needs. This may mean removing another person's photographs, name or address and replacing it with your own. Most good graphics software will allow you to do this ease.

Make sure you choose the correct type of paper to print on. ID cards are normally printed on thick card, whereas birth certificates are on fine paper. Ideally, your paper should be the correct weight, white and with no watermarks. Print out your fake; on both the back and the front, if required.

If your fake copy contains a watermark you will need to prepare the paper by embedding a watermark picture to the same density as that of the original. Most modern graphics programs allow you to do this. Simply choose your design, select the density and correct size and print. Use your watermarked paper to print out your fake copies.

The problem now is to process your new fake so that it looks like an original. If it is an ID card type, it will need trimming with a scalpel and sealing in a plastic protective jacket. Machines for doing this can be found in most major office supply stores. Once completed, always check your fake copy against a real one.

Age your document by placing a damp – not wet – cloth over the paper and iron over it several times. Next, place your document in the sun for several days. Once it has faded to your satisfaction, fold it several times then dust a little cigarette ash over the surface. Fold the paper several more times so that the ash falls into the creases. Your document is now ready; check your forgery against a real one once more.

Money can be made in the same way. However, to make an undetectable copy requires a great deal of skill. Once again, the secret lies in the choice of paper and in copying both the watermark and metal strip. One of the major problems of counterfeiting, especially bank notes, is the use of Radio Frequency Identification (RFID).

Radio Frequency Identification

RFID tags are regarded as either active or passive. Active RFID tags are powered by an internal battery and are typically used to track anything from pallets to dogs.

Passive RFID tags operate without a separate external power source and obtain operating power generated from the reader. Passive tags are consequently much lighter than active tags, are much cheaper to produce and offer an unlimited operational lifetime. One of their new uses is tracking bank notes around the world. The new European notes have the traditional metal strip, into which are placed two RFID tags. Each tag can trace its whereabouts from its origin to the present day. The absence of a tag means that the money is counterfeit. Similar tags can be found in ID cards, driving licenses and credit cards. You can always check where the tags are by placing your bank note in a microwave oven for about 30 seconds – the tags will "pop" and burn two small holes.

7 SABOTAGE

Sabotage can be carried out by any member of an intelligence agency. It can be a single act carried out by an agent or it can involve the destruction of major facilities by special forces. Operations that require demolitions or sabotage are commonly known as "bang-and-burn" operations. Although not always necessary, the use of explosives increases the effectiveness of sabotage.

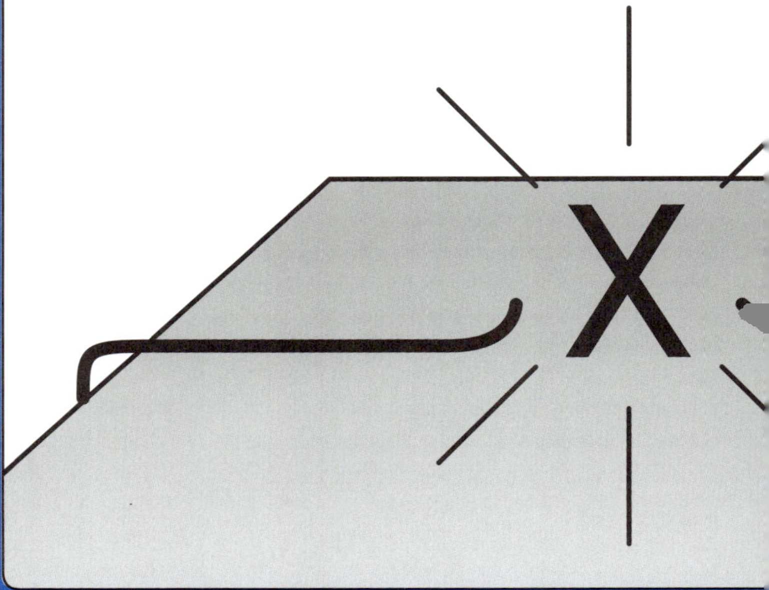

Finding and recruiting people to carry out sabotage depends on the individual situation. If a country is in rebellion and if special forces personnel are assisting the guerrillas with training, it is often best to get civilians to carry out small, non-explosive acts of sabotage. Students are particularly good for this. With a few exceptions, the students of most countries are at odds with the government over one issue or another; it is simply a matter of infiltration and organization to get them to work for you. The best method is to use an agent that is compatible with the student fraternity and to task them with defining the militant elements within the student movement. Once this is done, it is simply a matter of organizing student riots into which you can infiltrate your own guerrillas. Once the latter start the ball rolling, the riot will be self-perpetuating. The government will react predictably with over-zealous violence that will lead to an escalation of the riots and the use of petrol bombs etc.

Advisable Sabotage Techniques

There are hundreds of different types of sabotage technique, but all of the most successful share certain basic similarities. They should be relatively simple and quick to perform and be able to be undertaken without significant risk of exposure or capture.

Fell Trees in Road: While it might appear to be a simple task, felling a large tree in the right place can cause long delays and hold-ups. If these hold-ups include enemy troops, then you have created a perfect ambush area.

A Potato up the Exhaust: A simple potato rammed into an exhaust will stop any vehicle after a few metres. Make sure that you push it well up inside the tail pipe so that it is difficult to remove.

Sand or Sugar in Fuel: Placing sugar or sand in the fuel tank will stop a vehicle, although it will not do too much damage to the engine. Using treacle will cause the engine to seize totally.

Tyre traps: Old nails, twisted in such a manner that they fall spike up when dropped onto the ground (known as "jacks"), are ideal for bursting a vehicle's tyres. A well-planned ambush sight can stop a military convey – place your jacks at night and on sharp corners.

Create Waste and Drain Capital: In guerrilla warfare everyone can help by draining the government's resources. Leave taps running, smash and burst water pipes, bring down telephone lines, knock out the local electricity substations, burn vehicles in the street, create no-go areas for government troops etc.

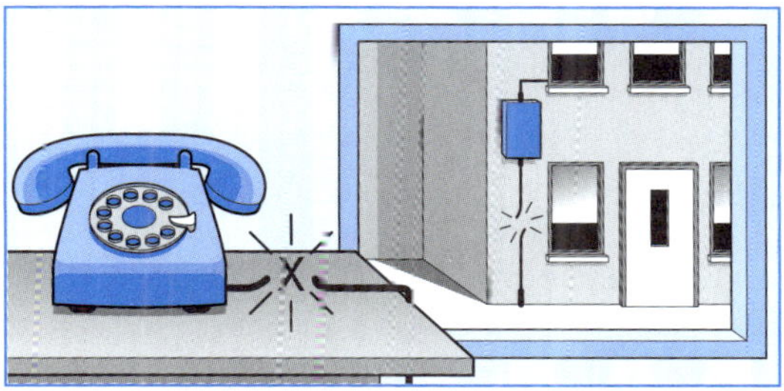

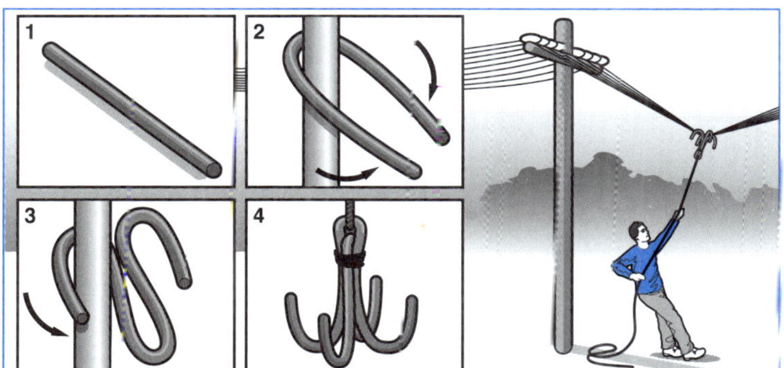
1
2
3
4

Cyber Sabotage

Many nations rely heavily on their economic infrastructure, much of which is entirely computer-based. However, this very reliance on computers also makes them vulnerable.

Computers support the delivery of goods and services, aid manufacturing, governance, banking and finance. What would happen say if the stock exchange computers were put offline for several days, or if the banks could not issue money to their customers because all of the accounts had been wiped out? While both would have a continuous back-up system, it is feasible that someone in the know could, after years of research, also find ways of destroying those as well.

All political, military and economic interests depend on information technology. This includes critical infrastructures such as electric power, telecommunications and transportation. The information technology infrastructure is at risk not only from disruptions and intrusions, but also from serious attacks.

The military, in particular, rely heavily on computerized weaponry. Smart bombs and cruise missiles are guided to their target via Global Positioning System (GPS), as are many of the ground troops. If you could find a way of shutting down the 27 or so satellites the system uses, the US military would be blind in one eye. What if someone could get both access to and control of the nuclear missile system?

The Internet

The invention of the Internet and email has, in general, advanced mankind in a huge way.

Information and basic knowledge on just about any subject is now available. Simply booking your holiday or sending flowers to your girlfriend can now be done with a few strokes of the keyboard. Billions of emails a week speed up conversation, save telephone charges and enable us to communicate rapidly around the world. Unfortunately, the price we must pay for this service is high, not in monetary cost, but in the way in which both the Internet and email can be exploiuted and abused.

The Internet offers unlimited facilities to the saboteur: from the knowledge on how to make home-made explosives and how to construct a bomb to any amount of information on a potential target. Email can be encrypted in such a way that no government agency can crack the code, thus allowing terrorist organizations secure communications on a worldwide basis. The same system allows them to contact other groups and to prepare joint operations. Business and bank accounts can be established over the Internet which provide money for weaponry and operations. If done properly, almost all these activities are untraceable.

8 HOSTILE ENVIRONMENTS

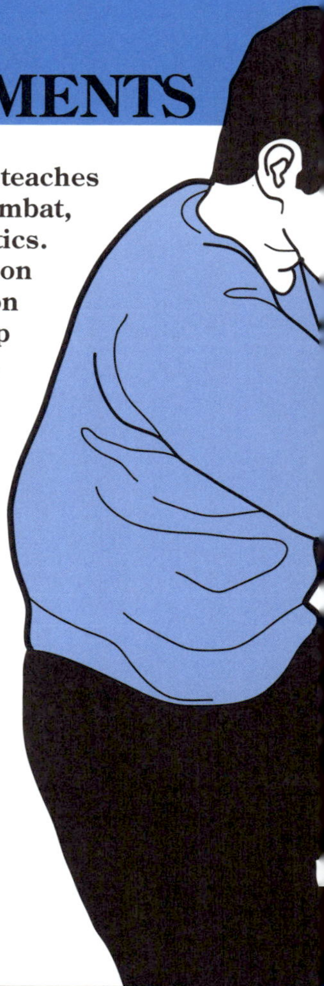

Hostile environment training teaches an individual about military combat, weapons, explosives and tactics. A modern spy must learn weapon safety drills, how the weapon operates and be able to field strip the weapon in an emergency. Once these skills have been mastered, the student will move on to basic shooting skills, movement and room clearance drills.

Disclaimer

All of the information and techniques in this section are for illustrative purposes only and none of them should be acted upon.

It is always useful for the spy to have a fundamental understanding of explosives and demolitions. A modern spy needs to know how to detect a bomb, deal with a bomb or how to make a bomb. In the normal case of events, specialist units, such as the SAS, will be brought in to perform demolition tasks. This unit has its own unique demolitions course that is restricted to the SAS officers only. The course teaches all the formulas for explosives, both commercial and homemade and their use in sabotage operations. British spies learn their basic skills during the IONEC military week, when they get to work with the Increment (a team of former SAS and Special Boat Service personnel who work for MI6).

They must also learn resistance to interrogation. If spies and agents get caught, the information that they possess may be of vital importance to the enemy – if captured, therefore, a spy can almost always expect to be tortured. The modern spy also needs to learn escape and evasion techniques, how to evade dogs and how to stay free once he has escaped.

While these are essential skills for the spy to acquire, his first and foremost skill must be to assess the threat. This means spotting a dangerous situation before it comes to fruition, dealing with a situation that has arisen, and escaping from that situation.

Awareness

When living and operating in a hostile environment, the spy has to live on his wits. He must be aware of suspicious people or actions that occur at his accommodation or his place of employ.

The spy must always be on the alert against an enemy attack. This requires vigilance, observing his immediate environment whenever he is awake. First and foremost, he must evaluate the geography of his location. For example: meeting and dealing with a group of thugs outside a pub in London may result in a good kicking; meeting a group of armed terrorist sympathizers in the back streets of Beirut will result in death. The list of awareness practice is inexhaustible, but here are a few guidelines.

- **Be aware of areas with a high-risk element.**
- **Maintain a fit state of mind – being drunk always makes you vulnerable.**
- **Change your routine, be unpredictable.**
- **If the traffic drives on the left, walk on the right-hand side of the road. This gives you plenty of time to observe vehicles coming towards you, but makes it difficult for any surveillance following you.**
- **Avoid observable patterns of behaviour that would enable the enemy to predict your future movements; change your eating and drinking places on a regular basis.**
- **Do not catch a bus or a train from the same stop or station every day.**
- **Never telephone for a taxi from your accommodation. The enemy may be listening in and may provide their own taxi. If meeting an agent get the taxi to drop you off several hundred metres away from your home. Then walk away in the opposite direction.**
- **Never reveal particulars of your movements to anyone you do not trust. Avoid pre-booking any travel. If you must pre-book, do so under someone else's name.**
- **When you are on public transport, seat yourself where you can observe the other passengers. Get a seat near to the door for a rapid escape.**
- **If you think you are being followed, get off and walk back the way you came. Check to see if anyone is following you.**

- **Have a back-up plan should things go wrong.**
- **Put your car in a garage if you have one.**
- **Have photographs of the cars that are normally parked outside in the street – check for any newcomers.**
- **If you must park on the road, park in a place where you can see it from your house.**
- **Fit a good motion detector alarm.**
- **If driving, keep your rear and side-view mirrors clean.**
- **Never leave articles in the vehicle, they can be booby-trapped.**
- **Never carry important documents in a briefcase; always carry them on your person and use the briefcase as a dummy.**
- **Keep away from dark or isolated areas, especially at night. Avoid walking through public parks late at night.**
- **If other people are in the vicinity, keep a few metres away from the nearest person if possible. This gives you time to react.**

Timing is also important. The same back street in Beirut may be a peaceful market place during the hours of daylight, with the bustling streets offering a degree of protection and normality. At 2 am, the market traders will have gone home and the street will be empty.

The first question the spy must ask himself is, "Why I am here?" Assuming you started in a safe location, why are you now in a hostile one? No one simply walks into danger, but the activities of a good spy may require him to do so. It may be that he is going to meet an agent, or that he needs to obtain information about a person or a property. In planning his task, he must understand the dangers both known and assumed, and make preparations for his safety. He needs to establish whether he should walk, drive, arm himself or have back-up units ready to assist.

The logic of both geography and time provides us with situation awareness; a spy must learn and react to it if he is to survive. Situation awareness is a mixture of visual and mental simulation triggers.

Example: Feeling – this is not a good situation. The area is known to be hostile. Normal activities have calmed down, i.e. the local population are moving for cover. Small groups of young men are gathering around loosely. You are the only stranger in the immediate vicinity. What do you do?

- **Ideally, at the first signs of a situation such as this, you should casually walk or drive to the last known safe area and extract yourself.**
- **If this is not possible, or if your way is blocked, you must look for an escape route.**
- **If none are available, prepare for an imminent attack, but keep moving.**
- **Aggressively confront those blocking your path.**
- **Fight and flee. (Aggressive Actions.)**
- **Call for hot extraction. (The problem with calling for back-up is that you blow your cover.)**

A "hostile situation" is a term that is often used very loosely. Basically, it implies that something, usually unplanned, has happened, and that you now find yourself in a totally unknown and unexpected environment from which there is no immediate prospect of extraction. If you are a suspected spy your life may now be under threat. Your physical fitness and your exact location at the time of awareness will to a large extent determine your reaction to any unplanned incident. The prospect of being killed or taken prisoner by an enemy must rank as one of the most frightening situations a spy must face. When the immediate fear of the unknown and the looming threat of death plays havoc with the emotions, the only channel open to the spy is to fight – and fight to win.

The Basics of Self-Defence

In the world of intelligence gathering, most premeditated attacks are normally carried out by religious zealots, many of whom are also under the influence of either drugs or alcohol.

As previously stated, the secret of avoiding any such attack is awareness and preparation. Awareness will take away the element of surprise from your attackers; preparation will help you defend yourself.

In any confrontational situation, stay calm and stay ready. Never allow reasonable behaviour to be mistaken for weakness. Defuse the situation by looking confident, always looking for avenues of escape. Remember, if your opponents have been drinking heavily or are under the influence of drugs, they will not be able to run very far before they are short of breath. If a fight looks imminent, get your blows in first, do it quickly and with all the aggression you can muster.

BALANCE

Fighting skills, no matter what form they take, all depend on one single factor, balance. We need to acquire the skill to be able to overcome any antagonist, to this end there is one outstanding principle: "Without balance there is no strength."

If your body is not properly poised, and thus unbalanced, any struggle between two unarmed people will rely on pure muscular exertions – which means the stronger person will win. In order to win against a stronger person, you must adopt a positive mental attitude, coupled with speed and aggression. The "on-guard" stance will automatically put your body into a well-balanced position from which you can use your body strength to its full advantage.

ON GUARD

Stand facing your opponent with your feet apart until they are about the width of your shoulders. Favour one leg slightly forward and bend your knees. Keep your elbows tucked in, and raise your hands to protect your face and neck. It is best to practice this move in front of a large mirror – stand relaxed and then, with a slight jump, go into the on-guard position.

Do not stiffen and try to feel comfortable. Tell your body that it is a spring at rest. First try using your hands; throw out your favoured hand in a blocking motion – at the same time automatically place the other hand in front of your lower face to protect your mouth and your nose, but do not obscure your vision. Next, imagine that someone is about to punch you in the stomach. Keep your stance, with elbows in tight and twist your shoulders from the waist. You will find that this puts the muscle of your forearm in a protective position, without having to move your feet or upsetting your balance.

To practise keeping your balance, move about the floor, first sliding one foot back and drawing the other one after it quickly, until, no matter how you move, you can always stop instantly in balance without shuffling your feet into position, but with clear-cut, precise movements. When you have to move, try to flow. Do not lift your feet, unless you intend to kick. Do not cross your legs or you will lose your stance. Move in the opposite direction to any attack. Practice your on-guard position with a partner attacking you.

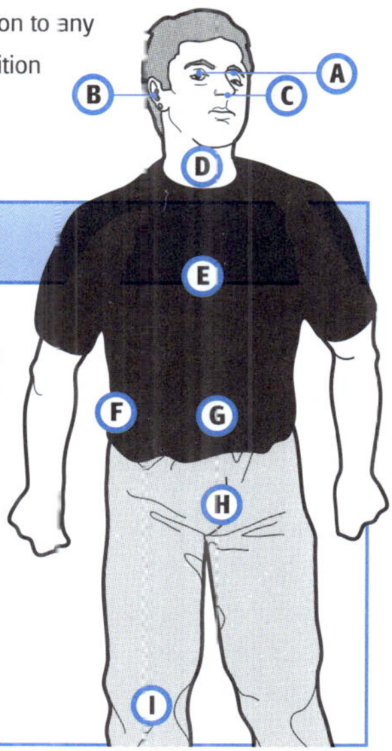

Vulnerable Parts of the Body

The human body is well adapted to taking punishment and will survive even the worst assault: this is one of the reasons we have progressed to the top of the animal chain. We can live with no arms or legs, without eyesight or without hearing, but life is a lot better with them. The most vulnerable parts of the body, are as follows.

A EYES
B EARS
C NOSE
D NECK/THROAT
E SOLAR PLEXUS
F KIDNEYS
G STOMACH
H GROIN
I KNEES

Eyes

We need our eyes, without them we are fairly helpless. Damage to an opponent's eyes will cause temporary, or even permanent, loss of vision. This will allow you to escape any attacker.

Ears

The ears offer a good target. They offer themselves readily available for you to bite. Sinking your teeth into someone's ear lobe will have the desired effect if you are being attacked. Clapping your open palms over both your attacker's ears will produce a rather nasty numbing sound to the brain, and has been known to cause unconsciousness. Jabbing a thin sharp instrument in the ear is potentially deadly.

Nose

Like the ears, it protrudes and therefore offers a good target to bite or strike with your fist. Feel free to use as much force as is deemed necessary to make your attacker break off the attack. Any upward blow will make the attacker lift his head and will offer his throat for a further attack. As with the ear, jabbing a thin sharp instrument up the nose can be potentially deadly.

Neck and Throat

The neck and throat can be very vulnerable. It also contains most of the vessels that keep us alive. Both of the main blood vessels that supply the brain are located close to the skin's surface on either side of the neck. Damage to either blood vessel can cause death. The airway is also easy to damage and a simple blow will incapacitate your attacker and give you time to escape. A single sharp blow to the back of the neck will cause a temporary blackout. Blows must be accurate and hard.

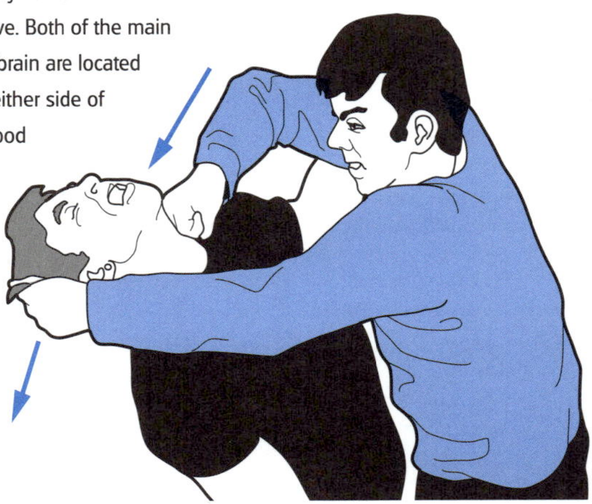

Delivering a Decisive Move

The secret of beating an opponent is to recognize the precise moment to strike. Sometimes just one blow, swift, sharp and accurate, driven home with all the power you can muster will suffice. Other times, you may need a practised set move. Assess your opponent's position and calculate your actions.

***Example:* In some cases, your attacker may block you against a wall and wait a few seconds before having a go at you. Should your attacker present himself side on to you at any time or if you can manoeuvre yourself into this position, take the following action:**

- **Grab the crown of his hair and pull his head back sharply.**
- **This will not only unbalance your attacker, but will expose his throat.**
- **Bring your fist up into his windpipe with one hard blow.**
- **If you continue to pull backwards, your attacker should drop to the ground.**
- **If your attacker has no hair to grip, use your hand like a claw and grab at his nose and eyes, forcing his head backwards.**
- **Once free, kick, break and run.**

Stomach and Solar Plexus

A heart punch, aimed at the point where the ribs start to separate, will have a devastating effect on any attacker. Likewise, most people do not have a muscle-bound stomach; the same blow delivered with force here will literally knock the wind out of a person.

Testicles

Although a good kick or blow to the groin will hurt a woman, it will cause triple the amount of pain to a man. It is also possible to grab and twist a man's testicles; while this procedure may repel a woman, it will produce the most amazing results.

Lower Legs

A backward blow against either knee joint is guaranteed to stop any attacker chasing after you. The legs are also a good area to kick when you are being held in a bear hug or if you are being gripped from behind. Stamping down hard on the attacker's toes will have the desired effect.

USING THE BODY FOR FIGHTING

When in conflict with an attacker, and if no other aid is available, you must rely on your own body in order to fight. Surprisingly, this is not as bad as it sounds, as the human body offers sufficient power and force to kill another human. However, this should only be a last resort and any fighting aid, no matter how insignificant, should be used in preference to the human body.

Balled Fist

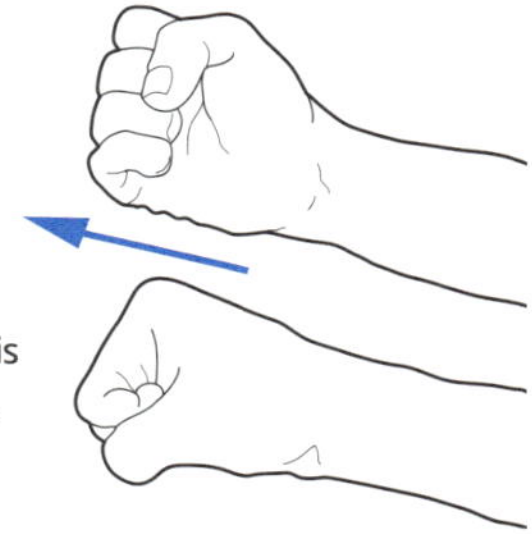

It is normal for the human to fight with a balled fist. Use your first punch to hit one of your attacker's vital target areas. Aim for the nose, chin, temple or stomach. If time permits, fill your hand with loose pocket change – this will increase the weight of any blow. Rain several blows in rapid succession and then try running off.

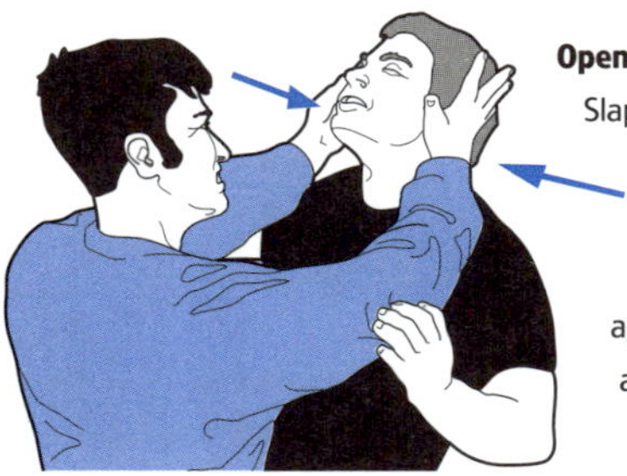

Open Palm

Slapping the open palms simultaneously against the ears, either from the back or from the front, will cause damage to your attacker. Using a chopping motion against the side and rear of the neck can also be very effective.

Heel of the Hand

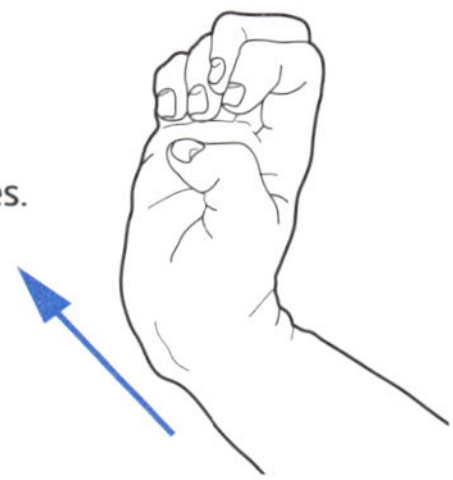

The chin jab is delivered with the heel of the hand, putting the full force of your body weight behind the punch. When attacking from the front, spread the fingers and go for the eyes. If attacking from the rear, strike the back of the neck just below the hairline for a very effective punch. As the head snaps forward, use your fingers to grab the hair and snap it back quickly. You are less likely to injure your hand if you use the heel-of-the-hand techniques.

Elbow

The elbow is a great weapon when you are side on or if you have your back to the attacker. Jabbing the elbow into your attacker's stomach will almost certainly drop him to the floor. If you have been knocked to the ground, try elbowing up into the testicles. Any well-connected blow from your elbow will give you enough time to break contact and run.

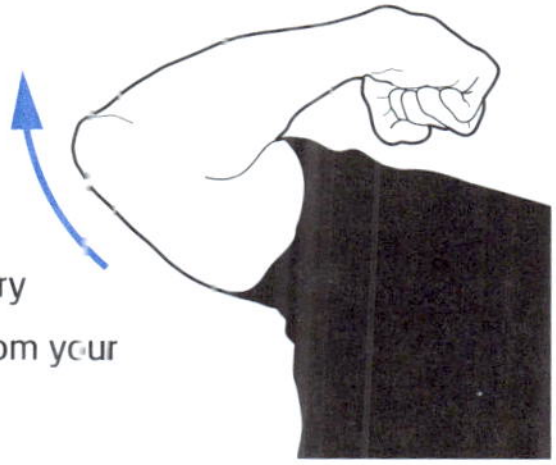

Knee

Although it is one of the body's more powerful weapons it is limited by its movement; it can only be directed to the lower part of your attacker's body. However its battering-ram effect can cause severe damage when driven into the testicles or when aimed at the outer thigh.

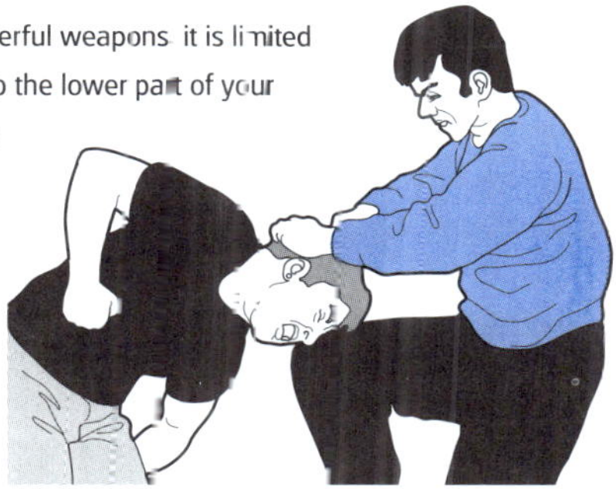

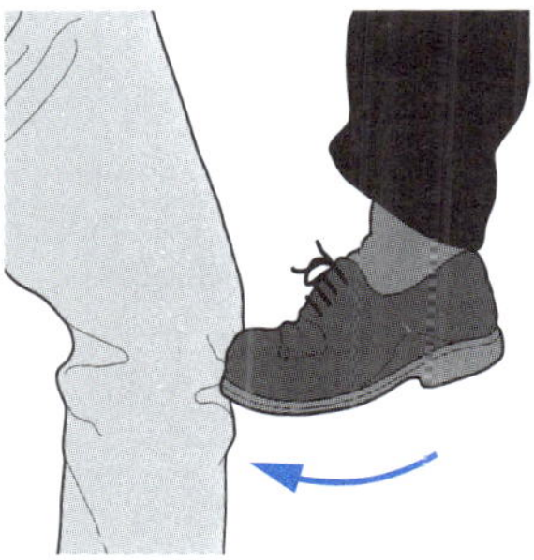

Foot

A hard kick is as good as any fist punch and can be used just as readily. Unless you have had some special training, keep your kicks below waist height. Remember, the moment you lift your foot from the floor, you become unbalanced.

Tip

There is an old saying in the SAS, "Take hold of a person's hair and the body will follow." The secret is to maintain your grip from the rear and never let your opponent twist around to face you.

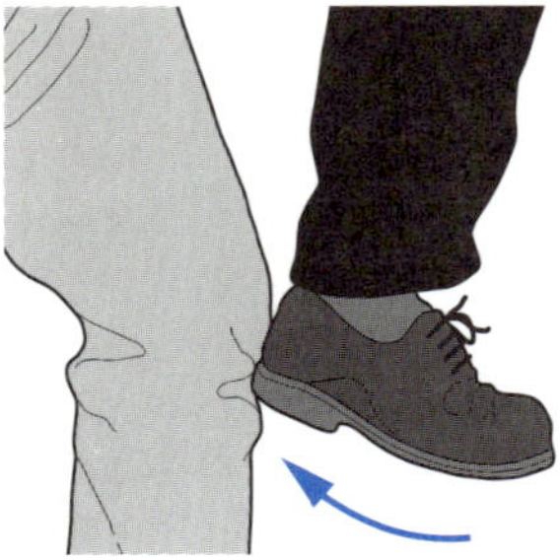

Heel

The heel can be an excellent self-defence tool if you have been grabbed from behind. Drive your heel down on to the instep of your attacker or stamp continually on his foot. Another effective way is to kick your attacker's anklebones.

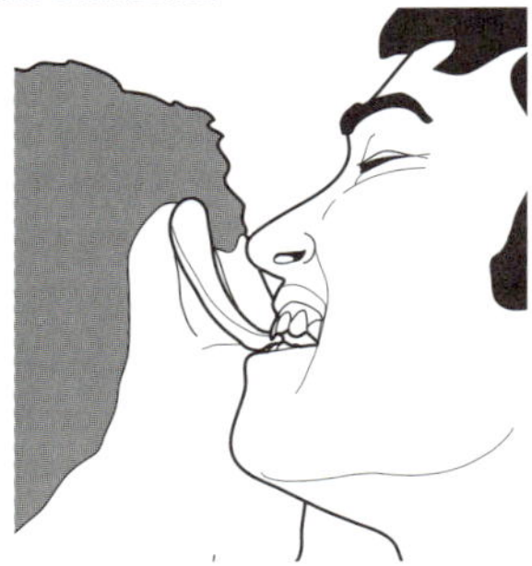

Teeth

Biting into any part of your attacker's body will cause severe pain and discomfort. The ears and nose are the best places to go for, but any exposed skin will do.

EVERY ITEM IS A WEAPON

While a spy may well be carrying a weapon, such as a pistol, circumstances may prevent him from using it. Likewise, the situation may not merit excessive force. For this reason, the spy must always carry a number of seemingly ordinary items that can be used as weapons.

Coins

Filling your hand with loose pocket change and forming a fist will greatly increase the force of any blow. Additionally, several coins tied into the corner of a handkerchief will form a very effective cosh. You can then swing it at the attacker's temple or general skull area.

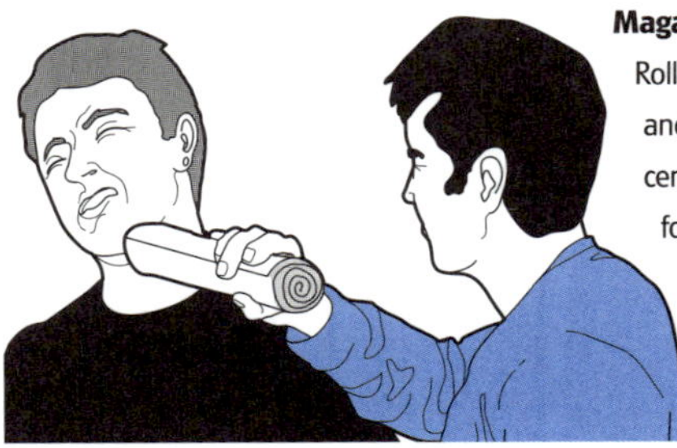

Magazine or Newspaper

Roll any magazine or newspaper into a baton and carry it around with you. Hold it by the centre to stab with, using either backward or forward thrusts. Hold the end of the baton if you intend beat your attacker around the head. A rolled-up newspaper is a great defensive weapon for fending off any knife attack.

Pen

Most types of pen have a pointed tip – that means that they will penetrate the skin if used in a punching manner. Hold the pen as if it were a knife and use it against any exposed part of the attacker's body, such as the neck, wrists and temple. The harder you punch with the pen, the better the results.

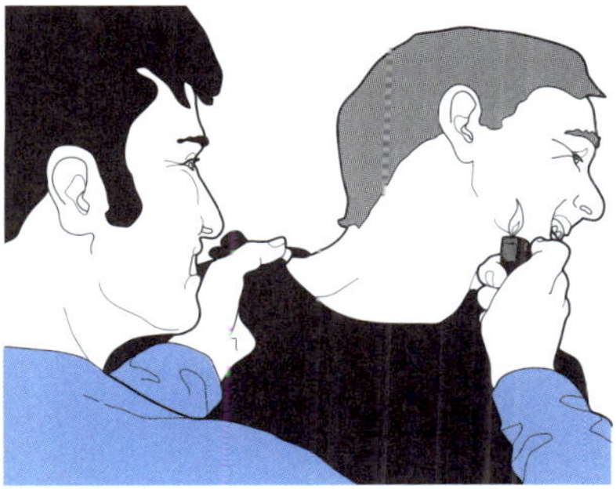

Ashtray

There is normally a plentiful supply of ashtrays in social premises some of which will be fairly full. Throw the ash into the attacker's face and follow up with the ashtray itself. Most ashtrays are round in shape and can be used as a Frisbee-type missile. A lighter can also make an effective weapon.

Bicycle

If you are attacked while riding a bicycle and cannot escape, pick the bike up and use it as a shield, in the same way as you would use a chair. The bicycle pump is also very handy to use.

Boiling Water

This is a good defence if you are attacked in your home. Boiling water splashed in the face will give you plenty of time to escape. Boiling water can come in any shape or form, a cup of hot coffee or tea or even hot soup. If you are in a restaurant, remember the coffee peculator.

Boots and Shoes

All your footwear should be comfortable but sturdy. Kicking is one of the basic defensive moves available to you, and it is no good trying to damage an attacker with a pair of flip-flops. A good solid boot will damage your attacker wherever you hit him. It is best to concentrate on the attacker's legs.

Belt Buckle

Any belt with a good metal buckle will provide a good defensive weapon. Wrap the tail end around your hand several times and then use the belt in a whipping action. Concentrate your attack on the exposed areas of skin, such as the face, the neck and the hands.

Chair

The common household or cafe chair is a very formidable weapon. Hold it by gripping the back support with one hand and the front of the seat with the other. Always try to attack with a chair if your attacker has a knife. The seat of the chair works as a shield, while the legs can be prodded into the attacker's head and chest.

Coat

This is not so much a weapon, but more of a shield. If you are attacked in the street, remove your coat and use it in the manner of a bullfighter. Throwing your coat over the attacker's head may only give you a couple of seconds head start, but you will run faster without it.

Deodorant Spray

Most women carry some form of spray in their handbag. Use it by spraying it directly into the face of any attacker. Hair spray is particularly effective against the eyes or when sprayed directly into the mouth or nostrils.

Caution: Some self-defence books advocate using a cigarette lighter to ignite the spray from an aerosol can. This will work, but it is also highly dangerous; there is more than a 50/50 chance that the can will explode in your hand.

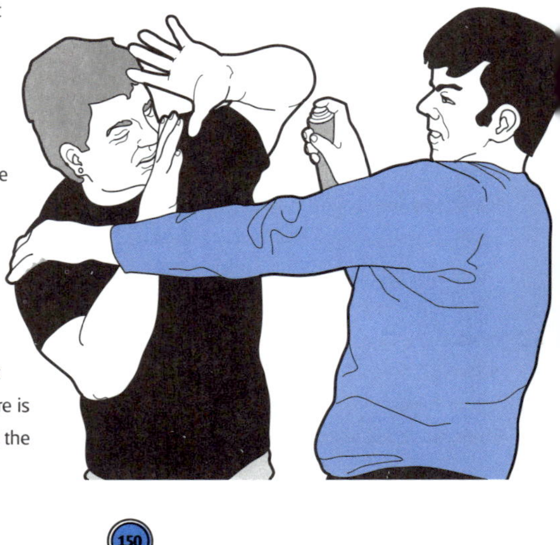

Fire Extinguisher

Most homes and offices now have several fire extinguishers. The pressurized contents can be used against any attacker by spraying him in the face. Once your attacker is blind, beat him over the head with the metal bottle.

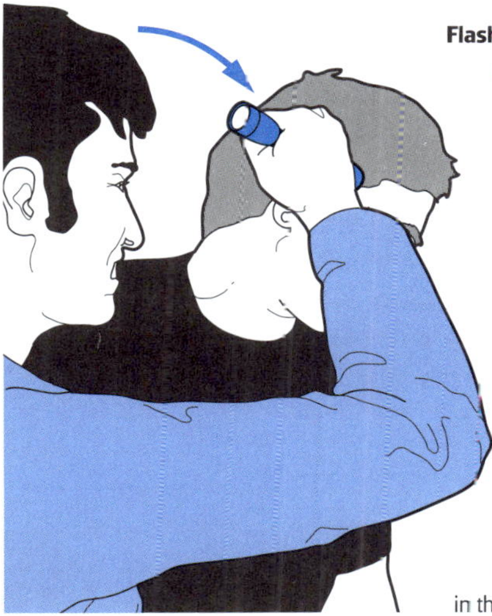

Flashlight

It is common sense to carry a flashlight with you while walking out any dark night. Although expensive, the more modern Mag-light type torches are extremely good and make an excellent weapon (the SAS have used them for years). Use the flashlight just as you would use a baton.

Keys

Most people carry a bunch of keys. Use them by laying the key-fob in the palm of your hand with the keys protruding between your fingers. This forms a very effect knuckleduster. Direct your blows against the vital pressure points of your opponent's head and neck.

Rocks and Soil

If you are attacked outdoors, throwing rocks at your attacker will help keep him at bay. Closer up, a handful of sand or dirt thrown in the attacker's face will temporarily blind him. The rock was one of man's first weapons.

Socks

Silly as it may seem, a sock will readily make a very effective cosh. Fill it with sand, chippings or soil. In the home, or if you are on the street, use loose pocket change. Swing it hard at the attacker's head in the same way as you would use any cosh.

MAKE YOUR OWN PROTECTION DEVICES

It is fairly easy to make a wide range of protective devices; most only require a little imagination. The secret is to make your protection as innocent as possible, that is to say, make it look like an everyday item. Once you have made your protection, try it out and make sure that it works the way you intended it to work.

Weighted Clothing

One of the best protective items is the cosh. There are several advantages to using a cosh; a hit in the right area with a well-made cosh will immobilize most attackers and they are easy to conceal. The ideal material for a cosh is lead, followed by copper or steel. Lead is cheap and can be purchased from most fishing accessory or DIY shops. It can be beaten into shape or smelted down and reformed into just about any configuration. As an alternative, use lead shot that is designed for air powered weapons. This is freely available from most hunting or sporting outlets. The metal can be used to weight clothes including the peak of a baseball cap and a tie.

Pepper Spray

Defensive sprays are banned in many countries. However, an effective, but non-lethal spray can easily be made. Both pepper and curry powder offer an excellent deterrent against attacks in the home. In an emergency, it is possible to throw the dry contents directly into the face of your attacker. A much better idea is to fill a plant spray bottle with a rich mixture of both ingredients and water. Two ounces of each, added to half a pint of warm water, is a good mix. Let the contents settle for a couple of days, giving it a good shake each morning. Keep your spray in a safe, but accessible place. Always keep it out of the reach of children.

Defensive Moves

If you are attacked from the rear and the attacker's arms or hands or within range, try biting them. If you manage to get your teeth into a section of his skin, only bite a small section. By doing this, you will get a better grip and it will hurt a lot more. A small section is also easier to rip at; grind your teeth into it and always try to come away with some flesh.

If your attacker has a low bear hug hold on you, with his arms more around your waist than your chest and thus making it difficult for you to slip out off, try doing a rear head-butt. Push up on your toes, bend forward at the waist – then slam your head sharply backwards.

Try to hit the attacker's nose. If an attacker grabs you from behind using just one arm, take the following action.

- **Push your bodyweight forward, twisting in the opposite direction of your attacker's gripping arm.**
- **At the same time, raise your left elbow as high as possible out in front of you.**
- **Your attacker will automatically try to pull you back. Use this by twisting back the opposite way, only this time use your momentum, and that of your attacker, to bring your elbow back into his face.**
- **This move can be combined with a backward blow from your other hand, driving your balled fist into his testicles.**

If you have been grabbed from behind in a bear hug with both your arms pinned at your side, do the following:

- **Bend your backside into the attacker; at the same time link your fingers together.**
- **Bend your knees to drop your body height and try to slip down through the bear hug.**
- **With your fingers linked swing your elbows out.**
- **Using a rocking, twisting movement, swing from the hips, driving your right elbow into your attacker's stomach.**
- **Follow through with a back head butt or a back instep foot stamp.**
- **Once free, kick, break and run.**

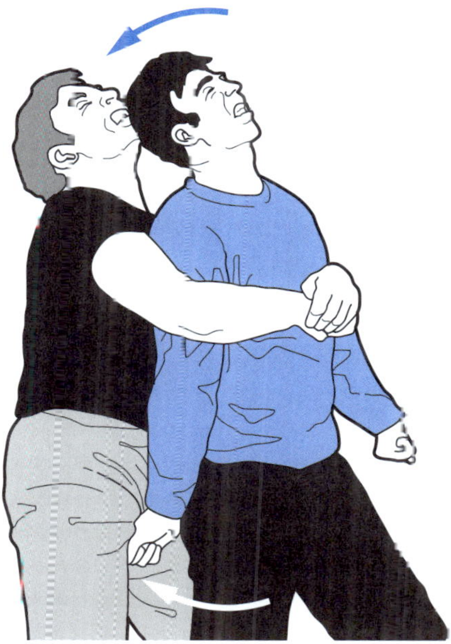

Most normal attacks start will start from the front. If you are quick and can recognize that you are about to be attacked, take the following actions before you are held:

- **Go into your fighting stance.**
- **Block with your left arm and punch or chin jab with your right hand.**
- **Continue through the motion. Push back the attacker's head to unbalance him.**
- **Make sure that you are well balanced before you bring your knee up into his groin.**
- **Try to avoid the attacker holding on to you or any part of your clothing.**
- **Once free, kick, break and run.**

In many instances, an attacker will grab you around the throat using both of his hands in a strangle hold. He will generally force you to the ground maintaining this hold. If possible, try to relax; the strangle hold on you will not be as effective. Should you find yourself threatened in this manner, take the following action:

- **In the early stages, when your attacker has just gripped you, bring your right hand, fist clenched, up to your left shoulder.**
- **With a backward swing, drive a back-fist against your attacker's temple (this can be a devastating blow).**
- **If this is not successful, link your fingers together between you and your attacker.**
- **Raise your clenched arms in an "A" above your head and then drive them down, maintain the "A" by keeping your elbows lower than your hands.**
- **This will have the effect of either breaking your attacker's hold or, at worst, bringing his head forward.**
- **Snap your forehead down on your attacker's nose as you bring your linked arms down.**
- **This procedure can be used either standing or lying down on the ground.**

KICKING

Learning to kick properly is not something that many people bother to study, but ask any marshal arts expert or a Thai boxer and they will advocate the advantages of giving your attacker a good kick. Your legs are much stronger than your arms and they can deliver a really powerful blow. The secret is to keep your kicks low; unless you have a clear line to an attacker's testicles, never kick above knee height. If you do, you are putting yourself off balance and possibly allowing your attacker to grab your leg, at which time he will have control over you. Direct kicks to the side of the ankle or to the front of the knee will always produce good results.

STEPS AND STAIRS

Sometimes you will be attacked on, or near, steps or stairs. If you are being chased or forced up a flight of steps, carry out the following actions:

- **Get in front of your attacker.**
- **Wait until you are near the top, then bend down and grip the top step or handrail.**
- **As you lean forward to do this, bend your knee and then kick back with your foot.**
- **Your hit should be around chest height; using this, try to knock your attacker down the stairs. Chase after him and continue kicking until you can make good your escape.**

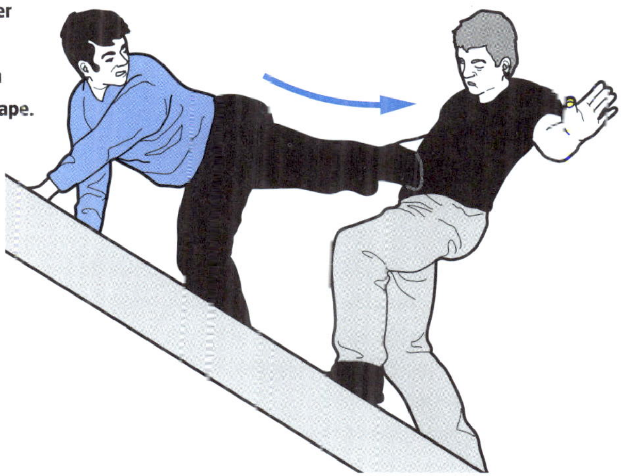

GETTING UP FROM THE GROUND

Learning the art of falling is almost as important as staying on your feet, but the chances are that at some stage during a conflict you will get knocked to the ground. Therefore, it is something that you need to practise. Falling in the gym on mats is vastly different from being thrown onto the road or rough ground. Once down you become vulnerable, but not helpless. It is possible to fight from the ground, but my advice is toget up as soon as possible.

This is the method to use to get up from the ground. All moves should be made in one continuous roll of your body:

- **Turn over sharply onto your left side, with your stomach facing downwards.**
- **Place both palms on the ground and push. At the same time, tuck your right knee under your body.**
- **Swing your left leg under your body until your foot is flat on the ground.**
- **Spring up and turn to face your attacker.**
- **Adopt the on-guard position.**

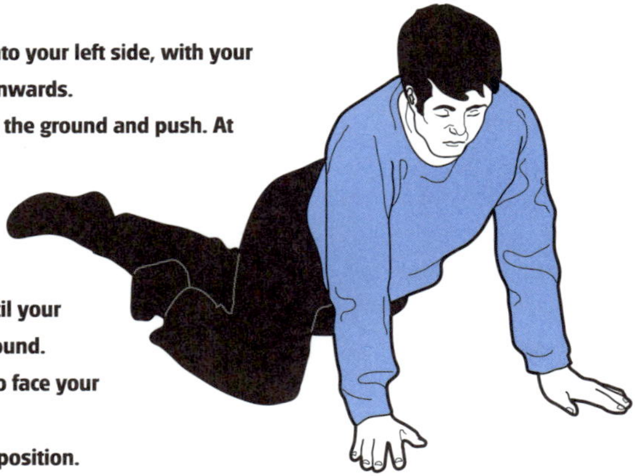

You may have seen the following method in a lot of movies, but with a little practice it will work:

- **Roll onto your back.**
- **Bring your knees up to your chest and over your head in a rocking motion.**
- **Rock forwards using a rolling action.**
- **Favour either your left or right hand and place your palm down to spring back onto your feet.**
- **Face your attacker.**
- **Adopt the on-guard position.**

DEFENDING AGAINST WEAPONS

Guns, knives and machetes are all very dangerous weapons – in most close-range attacks, they will cause serious injury, or even kill. In the event of a robbery, give up your possessions without any fuss. In the event that you are a suspected spy, you may have little choice other than to defend yourself. In truth, unless you are fully trained and confident in dealing with such situations, your chances are slim.

It is very difficult to offer any defence against a person who is holding a gun on you. If someone is carrying a gun, you have to assume that he will use it. An automatic pistol normally has a magazine that contains a certain amount of bullets. The magazine needs to be in the pistol; it normally fits inside the handgrip. Once in position, a bullet has to be fed into the chamber of the barrel. This is done when the top slide is pulled back, cocking the pistol. At this stage, providing the safety catch is off, the weapon will fire if the trigger is squeezed.

A revolver is different in as much as it houses its bullets in a round cylinder. When the trigger is pulled, a bullet is fired and the cylinder is moved one place to the right, thus pulling a new bullet under the hammer ready to be fired.

There are techniques for disarming a person that is holding a gun on you, but these take years of practice and even then there is no guarantee that they will work. In the event that you are being threatened with a gun, and your death, or the death of another looks imminent, try to take the following actions.

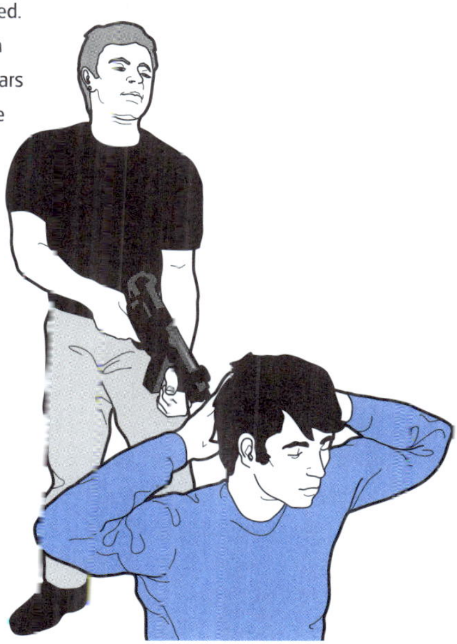

- **Assess the person holding the gun. Could you take him if he was unarmed?**
- **Assess his actions. How close does he come to you? (A professional will keep out of striking range.)**
- **Look at the weapon. Is it an automatic or a revolver? Is the firing hammer cocked back?**
- **Can you see if the safety catch is in the on or off position?**

With the gunman standing in front of you and with your hands in the air, a straightforward downward snatch at the gun with both hands may work. Once you have hold of the gun, grip it for all you are worth, use both hands to twist the gun away from you and towards your attacker.

He will think twice before pulling the trigger. Given that you have a good leverage on the barrel of the weapon, you may be able to wrestle it from your attacker's hands. If you get hold of the weapon, or if it falls free, kick it or throw it out of range and continue your fight on a more even basis.

Both automatic pistols and revolvers will only fire a bullet that is in the chamber, immediately under the hammer. It is possible to prevent a second bullet being fired by holding the top slide of an automatic pistol or by gripping the cylinder of a revolver.

If your gunman has his weapon pressed into your back and you are standing still, try twisting your body around suddenly when you feel the weapon pressed in your back. Use a back-fist blow to block the attackers weapon hand. Follow through with a really aggressive action. Grip and hold the weapon hand to stop the attacker from firing the gun. Remove the weapon from your attacker's grip if possible.

If you manage to disarm your attacker temporarily, pick up the weapon. If you are unable to do this, put some distance between yourself and the gunman. Even 20 metres will suffice; it is almost impossible to hit a running man at this distance with a pistol. Zigzag, as you run.

Do not stop even if you feel a bullet hitting you; if you are seriously hit, you will go down automatically. Put at least 50 metres between yourself and the gunman; his aim may not be very good, but a lucky bullet can still kill you.

Full Automatic Weapons

By nature, spies often operate in areas that are termed "unstable", that is to say areas in which there is some degree of violence. It is a sad fact of life that such areas are also flooded with automatic weapons. In most cases, these weapons are used by untrained and undisciplined people, many of whom are little more than children. Automatic weapons are used in war zones and for serious crimes, such as drugs and terrorist activities.

If you are confronted by anyone with an automatic weapon, do exactly what they say. The only true defence against an automatic weapon is to be armed yourself and to shoot first.

Knife Attack

There are two types of knife attack. The first is committed by someone who is in dispute with you and a knife happens to be handy. This type of person is not likely to stab or cut you, but will intend to use the knife in a threatening manner. This can be a good stage at which to call a halt to the conflict, by convincing the attacker of the consequences if he stabs you. This may not work, but people who are not used to fighting with a knife will sometimes listen to reason. In some instances, the attacker may use a knife to equal the odds, as he sees it, against a larger or more aggressive opponent. In this case, let the aggressor know exactly what you will do with the knife if you get hold of it. Most will back down at the thought.

The degree of threat is related to the weapon and to the skill of the person using it. If you are involved in a conflict with a person who normally carries a knife, back down. Try to avoid the situation and run away if you can. Knives can, and often do, kill; if you are forced to fight, carry out the following actions

- **Look for a blocking object, such as a chair.**
- **Get some protection around one arm, such as a jacket or a coat.**
- **Stay away from the knife if your attacker is slashing.**
- **If he is using a stabbing action, take the blade on a padded arm.**
- **Use a stick, a broom or an umbrella to parry the knife hand.**
- **Do not try to kick the knife hand, go for the attacker's lower legs.**

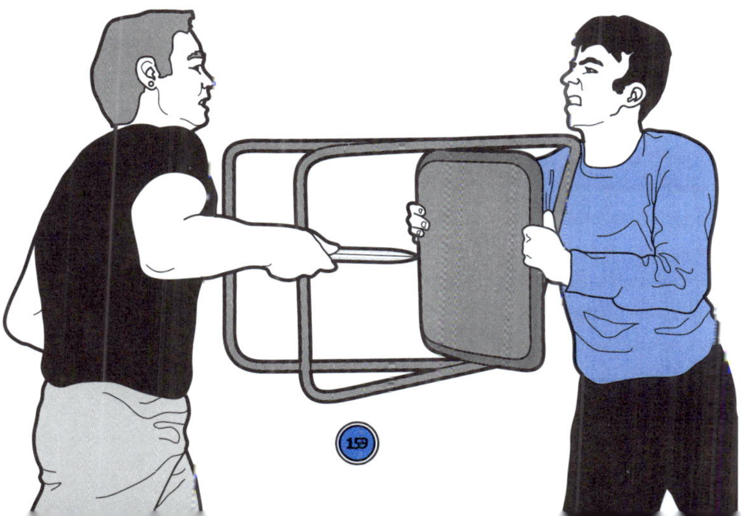

DOGS

The threat of dogs can come from two directions. First, your presence in an area could be compromised by domestic dogs; the second, and by far the biggest threat, is the detection, pursuit and capture by professional tracker dogs and their handlers.

Police or military dogs must conform to certain requirements, irrespective of their breed. They are physically strong, weighing between 50 to a 100 lb, with a good turn of speed over short distances. This basically means that they can run faster than a human and, if asked, take them to the ground.

The best type of dog should have a good temperament, be intelligent, courageous, faithful and energetic. The following breeds fit this category: Alsatians, Dobermanns, Rottweilers, Mastiffs and Labradors.

Sensory Characteristics

A dog relies very little on its sight during day-to-day activities; its attention is aroused by movement, and, if it is interested by it, it will then make use of its hearing and smell. There is no evidence that a dog's night vision is any better than that of a man, although its low position to the ground may help, as it will give objects a better definition.

A dog's hearing is twice as sensitive as that of a human, and a dog can be attracted by a noise that its handler cannot hear. However, its sense of hearing may well be governed by the weather, in particular wind and rain.

Dogs also have an amazing sense of smell. It is estimated to be some seven to nine hundred times greater than that of humans. It can track microscopic traces of a substance, or vapour that lingers in the air, on the ground or that has come into contact with other objects. A dog can also detect minute disturbances on the ground that may alter the "scent picture".

The Scent Picture

The scent picture is analyzed in two ways: from the "air scent" and from the "ground scent". Air scent comprises mainly of an individual's body scent, clothing, deodorants, toiletries and the chemical aid that is used when washing clothes. The total amount of body scent given off by a human will depend on his constitution, the activity he is undertaking and his mental state. As a prisoner runs along, this scent is suspended in the air for a short while before falling to the ground.

From the dog's perspective, the ground scent deposited will consist of two pictures: the body scent and the disturbance made in the environment as each foot hits the ground. This results in crushed vegetation, dead insects and the breaking of the ground's surface, which releases a gas vapour. Ground scent can last up to 48 hours or even longer in ideal conditions.

Certain factors will affect the scent picture: moist ground conditions, vegetation, humidity, forest areas and light rain mist or fog will all act to make favourable scent picture. Unfavourable conditions include arid areas, sand, stone roads and city streets, high winds and heavy rain.

The Guard Dog

Guard dogs are normally employed to detect intruders, locate them and physically apprehend them. In other words, they are used to protect both the property and the handler. They can be employed in several different ways:

- **Loose in a compound.**
- **On a running wire.**
- **On a lead with their handler.**

The Tracker Dog

The tracker dog is employed to find and follow a prisoner's scent as he progresses on foot. They work mainly on ground scent, unlike a guard dog that would work primarily on air scent.

The dog will normally follow the freshest scent. A lot will depend on teamwork between the dog and the handler. The dog is trained to follow a distinct track; it is up to the handler to ensure that it follows the correct one.

Dog Evasion

If a dog has spotted a moving man, it may lose interest if the man freezes. In immediate pursuit the only thing you can do is defend yourself. In a delayed pursuit, even if the delay is very short, there are several counter-measures that can be taken. Your main aim is to increase the distance between yourself and the dog. This can be helped in a number of ways:

- **Run steadily.**
- **Climb up or jump down vertical features.**
- **Swim rivers.**
- **If you are in a group, split up.**
- **Run downwind.**
- **Do things to confuse the handler.**

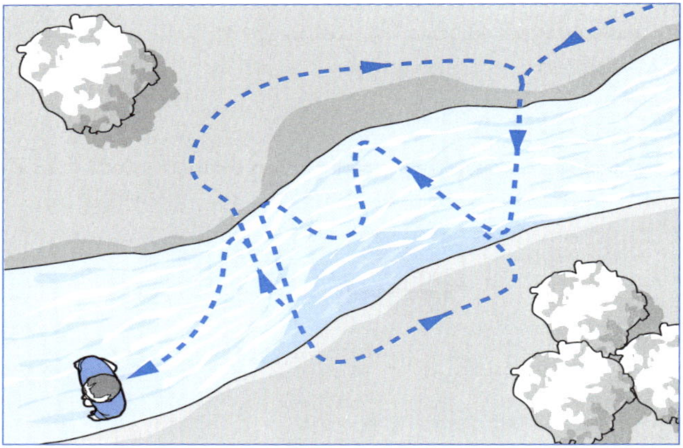

Note: If you are being tracked by a dog and its handler, you should cross an obstacle, say a river, and walk some 200 metres downstream and cross back over. If this pattern is repeated several times, the handler will think the dog has lost you and call the dog off. In reality, all you have done is confuse the handler.

Defense Against a Charging Dog

If a dog is charging at you, try to break the momentum that it will need to knock you to the ground. This can be achieved by standing next to an object like a tree until the dog is just a few feet away. Move rapidly behind the tree at the last moment. The dog will be forced to slow in order to turn. Take advantage of this.

Attacked by a Dog

An attacking dog will attempt to paw down any barrier placed in front of it; using a strong stick to bar his path could help. The dog will normally wish to take a bite and "lock on" to you. If this is the case, offer a padded arm to the dog. Once the dog has taken a grip, stab it in the chest or beat it on the head with a rock or a stick. Make sure that whatever you do to the dog, the injuries caused are permanent otherwise it will just become even more annoyed. If the handler is not present and you have no other weapon, try charging directly at the dog with your arms outstretched and screaming. Given the size of a human being in regards to that of a dog, and the sudden unexpected nature of the attack the dog may break. A dog's confidence and security can be weakened very quickly.

Do not try to use any chemical substances, such as pepper, to put the dog off the scent, as this will only increase the scent picture. If cornered by both dog and handler, it is best to give yourself up unless you are armed.

9 SELF-PRESERVATION

At the end of the day, the spy – just like any other individual – must be prepared to take responsibility for his or her own self-preservation. The world we all live in has more than its fair share of dangers, but the taking of a few regular, common sense precautions can greatly minimise a whole range of threats – from assassination to being the victim of violent crime. In a world where information is increasingly the key to survival, the techniques of self-preservation can now rest as much on protecting our personal data as our physical bodies.

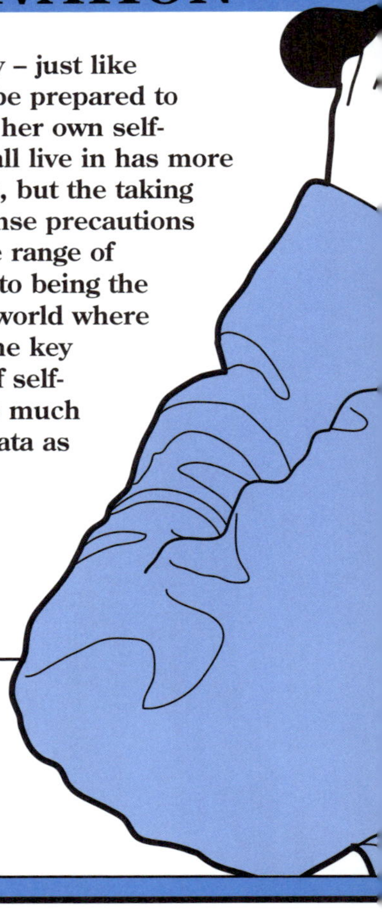

Security in the Home

Remember that you are at your most vulnerable when approaching or leaving your home. Anyone looking for you will know that at one time or another you can always be found there. Home is where you relax and drop your guard; it is also a place where you hold most of the documents and information that establish your identity.

Home is also a place you share with your loved ones. Keep this in mind and anticipate any intrusion into your personal life and home. Above all, always, always, listen to your senses and gut feelings – if something does not feel right, then it usually isn't. In the meantime, think about the following:

- **Get a dog with attitude. Better still, get two.**
- **If permitted, always have some form of weapon handy. A baseball bat is a good option.**
- **Construct a safe room within your house. Make this impregnable for at least five minutes. Make sure that you can activate an alarm from this room and that you have means to telephone the police.**
- **When not in use, make sure your car is always garaged, even in the day time.**
- **Always lock your garage and set the alarm.**
- **Fit sensor-activated cameras and record all activity around your home.**
- **Fit a very noisy alarm system.**
- **Fit deadlocks to all outer doors.**
- **Fit wrecker bars to glazed doors and windows.**
- **Protect weak and vulnerable entry points with magnetic contacts or glass-breaker sensors.**
- **Don't leave keys around the house. Use a key box for all of your keys and make sure you know who holds any keys to your home.**
- **Fit lightproof curtains to all windows. This avoids assassination from outside at night.**
- **Fit good lighting to all dark areas around the house.**

- **Always leave a light burning at night.**
- **Have emergency spot lighting that is controlled from inside the house.**
- **Have emergency lighting, such as gas lanterns and torches, easily accessible inside the house.**
- **Make entry and exit difficult for any assailant, with the aid of a high fence or a wall around the garden.**
- **Remove any house number and your name from the letterbox.**
- **Never answer the door automatically – always check who is there first.**
- **Put a chain on your door.**
- **Insist on seeing identity cards from anyone who needs access to your home, such as meter readers. Always ring their office to check they are who they claim to be.**
- **Never leave your home while strangers are present.**
- **Always lock your doors and windows, even if you are only leaving for a few minutes.**
- **Ask friends to telephone you before coming over.**
- **Treat all visitors, after midnight, as suspicious.**
- **If you are leaving your home for any length of time, cancel any regular deliveries.**
- **Have a trusted neighbour empty your mailbox.**
- **Never tell anyone about your business or the fact that you are going away.**

Preparation is the key to protecting both yourself and your family, but you cannot live under constant fear. I have found it advantageous to anticipate the types of attack that may be directed against my family and our home. For example, shooting involves line of sight, even for a sniper, and a person using a pistol needs to get within a few feet of you to be certain. Therefore, you are fairly safe when you are in your home. An explosive attack is more likely to be against your car, but letter bombs delivered to your home are also very effective. In some countries, there is a real hazard from potential suicide bombers, not just in the home but also while you are out socializing. A professional assassin will almost certainly get you, so there is little point in getting paranoid, just be aware, take a few simple precautions and follow your gut feelings.

I no longer keep sensitive material in my home, but, as a writer, I do hold a lot of valuable material. Both sensitive and valuable material should be protected. The best idea is to invest in wall safe and most DIY stores now stock a wide variety of them. Use a box folder for such things as family identification, birth certificates marriage certificate, passports etc, and another for any personal papers that you deem to be sensitive or valuable. Place these in a safe place under lock and key. Only remove them when necessary and avoid doing so when strangers are in your home. Never keep sensitive material that you no longer require in your home – destroy it. It is best to burn documents and then flush the ashes down the toilet.

Always back up any important material from your computer. Personally, I use a removable hard drive, rather than discs and remove this every night. Make sure that this hard drive is put in a safe, dry place. Computers are vulnerable to attack and it is a simple matter for people to hack into it and download all your information. Additionally, your computer stores a record of all your activities, including everything you download from the Internet. I purge my computer by formatting the internal hard drive every four to six weeks. While this may seem a little drastic, it works. I use my back-up hard drive to reinstall my important work. If you send an email, always make sure that it is encrypted and send important documents hidden within a digital picture (see Secret Codes).

While many telephones are fitted by private companies, most telephone systems are controlled by the State. This means that the State can listen to your conversation at any time. Additionally, your telephone can be bugged or used to trigger another hidden bugging device in your home. Use your home telephone as little as possible and never for important business. Always assume that a third party is listening in to your conversation as that way, you will not say anything you should not. Take the telephone apart and check if it has been tampered with, although it is almost impossible to tell these days. Keep a separate, "clean" telephone locked away and only plug this in when you need to talk to someone special. I purchased a mobile phone and several different SIM cards; making sure all of these are unregistered.

We all receive mail. For the most part we open the letterbox, take out the mail and open it in our homes – bad move. Letter bombs are easy to make, yet most people never give this a second thought. Most of us recognize our mail, the familiar bank statements, bills and volumes of junk mail. Occasionally there is one that stands out; it looks interesting and so we rush to open it. I always consider there may be a bomb-related risk. Ask yourself whether you were you expecting this letter. Do you know who sent it? Is the letter bulky, more than two sheets of writing paper? Do you feel any lumps or hard pieces through the envelope? If you are not sure, but do not want to look an idiot – here is a little trick.

Use a very thin piece of wire and carefully push it through the bottom of the envelope. Loop the wire and fasten a length of string to the loop. Most letter bombs only contain a small amount of explosive, so a three-metre length of string should be enough. Lay the envelope on the ground and secure it carefully with a weight – not enough to crush the letter, though. Then, from a safe distance, pull the wire that will rip open the bottom of the envelope. If it does not go bang, pick up the letter, bottom uppermost and investigate the contents. Many letter bombs are activated by the top flap being opened or by the contents being removed. You assess both of these methods by opening the bottom of the letter. Always be suspicious of bulky greeting cards that have musical chimes.

Remember that your car is an extension of your home. It is the means by which you travel to and from your home. This makes it equally vulnerable to attack. Many people have been killed by car bombs and there will doubtless be many more. It is a destructive form of attack and one that is fairly simple to achieve. Car bombs can be triggered by pressure, pull, speed, breaking or any electric device within the car, such as turning the radio on. They can also be triggered by various radio devices that are remote from the car. Always follow these basic rules to minimize the threat.

Most assassins who use car bombs always place the explosive close to the driver's seat, so make sure that you always check this area thoroughly. Always garage your car when it is not being used. Always check your car before getting in. Check the bonnet, underneath the car and under the seat. Go to both windows and look at the opposite door for signs of tampering or for any wires. Carry out a sweep every time you use your car, because if you are under observation this approach will often deter anyone from planting a bomb. Remember that the enemy can attack your car in four different ways:

- **Using a device placed directly on your vehicle that is detonated on entry or ignition.**
- **Using a device placed on the vehicle that is detonated while in transit by radio control.**
- **Placing a large bomb along the route you will travel – in a drainage ditch or on an embankment.**
- **By firing a rocket-propelled grenade at your vehicle.**

Finally, if you ever get attacked in your home and manage to gain the advantage over your assailant, make sure that you are aware of the legal status of any subsequent actions that you take to apprehend or prevent the assailant from being able to repeat their attack against you in the future.

APPENDIX

Bibliography

References and facts in this book were ascertained from the following sources:

Adams, James; *The New Spies*; Hutchinson 1994.

Andrew, Christopher & Gordievsky, Oleg; *KGB: The Inside Story*; Hodder & Bamford, James; The *Puzzle Palace*; Sidgwick & Jackson 1983.

Bar-Zohar, Michael & Haber, Eitan; *Quest For The Red Prince*; Weidenfeld & Nicolson 1983.

Davis, Simon; *Big Brother*; Pan 1996.

Geraghty, Tony; *The Irish War*; Harper Collins 1998.

Hagar, Nicky; *Secret Power*; Craig Potton Publishing 1996.

Harclerode, Peter; *Secret Soldiers*; Cassell & Co. 2000.

Hollingsworth, Mark & Norton-Taylor, Richard; Blacklist: *The Inside Story of Political Vetting*; Hogarth Press 1988.

Hollingsworth, Mark & Fielding, Nick; *Defending The Realm*; André Deutsch 1999.

Jenkins, Peter; *Advanced Surveillance*; Intel Publishing 2003.

Melman, Yossi & Raviv, Dan; *The Imperfect Spies*; Sidgwick & Jackson 1989.

Stoughton 1991.

Porter, Bernard; *Plots and Paranoia*; Unwin Hyman 1989.

Ranelagh, John; *The Agency*; Sceptre 1988.

Urban, Mark; *UK Eyes Alpha*; Faber & Faber 1996.

In addition, many of the techniques found within this book can be examined in greater detail by obtaining the following American Military publications.

FM 31–21	*Guerrilla Warfare And Special Forces Operations*
TM 31–210	*Improvised Munitions Handbook*
FM 5–31	*Booby Traps*
FM 34–40–5	*Voice Intercept Operations*
FM 34–54	*Technical Intelligence*
FM 2–27	*Intelligence Reach Operations*
FM 34–25–1	*Joint Surveillance Target Attack*
FM 34–44	*Signal Intelligence*
FM 34–5	*Human Intelligence And Related*
FM 34–52	*Intelligence Interrogation*
FM 34–56	*Imagery*
FM 34–7	*Intel Sup To Support Ops And Stability Ops*
FM 2–22–7	*Tactical Human Intelligence And Counter*
FM 34–8–2	*Intelligence Officer's Handbook*
FM 2–33–6	*Military Intel Command And Control*
FM 2–50	*Intelligence Systems*
FM31–21	*Guerrilla Warfare & SF Ops*
FM90–8	*Counter Guerrilla Operations*
FM31–20	*Special Forces Operations Doctrine*
FM31–20–5	*Special Forces Recon Tactics*
FM23–10	*Sniper Training*
TC23–14	*Sniper Training & Employment*
FM100–20	*Military Ops In A Low Intensity Conflict*
FM34–36	*Special Ops Intel & Electronic Warfare*
FM21–150	*Combatives*
FM21–75	*Combat Skills*
FM21–76	*Survival Evasion And Escape*

Index